MONTANA HISTORY FOR KIDS IN 50 OBJECTS

With 50 Fun Activities!

in cooperation with the
Montana
Historical Society

by **Steph Lehmann**

FARCOUNTRY
PRESS

Montana Historical Objects

Learn about Montana history with 50 objects from the Montana Historical Society—and have fun with 50 activities, plus five journaling pages to record objects you see here in the Treasure State!

Numbers in a ⬤ on the map match the object numbers in the Table of Contents, showing you where the 50 objects are from.

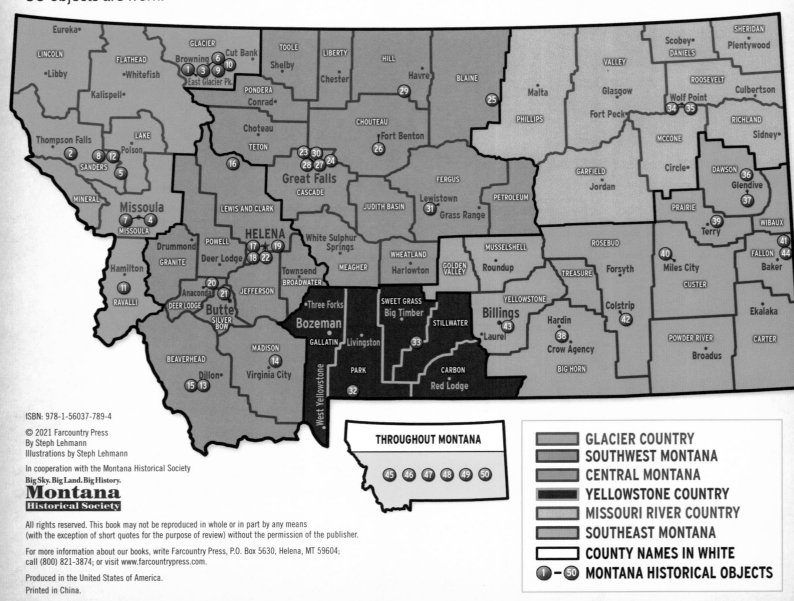

ISBN: 978-1-56037-789-4

© 2021 Farcountry Press
By Steph Lehmann
Illustrations by Steph Lehmann

In cooperation with the Montana Historical Society

Big Sky. Big Land. Big History.
Montana
Historical Society

For more information about our books, write Farcountry Press, P.O. Box 5630, Helena, MT 59604; call (800) 821-3874; or visit www.farcountrypress.com.

Produced in the United States of America.
Printed in China.

25 24 23 22 21   1 2 3 4 5

THROUGHOUT MONTANA
45 46 47 48 49 50

⬤ GLACIER COUNTRY
⬤ SOUTHWEST MONTANA
⬤ CENTRAL MONTANA
⬤ YELLOWSTONE COUNTRY
⬤ MISSOURI RIVER COUNTRY
⬤ SOUTHEAST MONTANA
☐ COUNTY NAMES IN WHITE
① - ㊿ MONTANA HISTORICAL OBJECTS

Table of Contents

Mountain Goats

When he was two years old, John L. Clarke lost his hearing due to scarlet fever, which also affected his ability to talk. He was known as *Cutapuis,* which means the Man-Who-Talks-Not in the Blackfeet language. Although he knew both American and Native sign language, he communicated best with his carvings—especially those of the wildlife in and around Glacier National Park. *Mountain Goats* is a masterpiece carved from a single piece of cottonwood. He used a variety of tools and techniques to capture the goats' shaggy hair and the texture of the rocks.

Clarke was born in 1881 in the town of Highwood in Chouteau County. From an early age, he was sent to schools for the deaf, some as far away as Wisconsin. Although he was separated from his family, the schools taught him skills for living a productive and creative life. In 1913, he returned to Montana and set up a small art studio in Midvale, today's East Glacier. He carved the animals he loved and knew from hiking and hunting in the area. He became well known for capturing not only an animal's anatomy but also its spirit. Many people collected his sculptures, from President Warren Harding to cowboy artist Charles M. Russell, as well as countless visitors to Glacier National Park. He was widely admired for his artistic ability and his genuine kindness. Unfortunately, much of Clarke's work was destroyed in a home fire in 1962. Luckily, his work lives on in collections like the one at the Montana Historical Society, where these two mountain goats will forever gracefully climb a mountainside.

Color the mountain goats

Draw and color the landscape you think the goats would be in.

Embroidered Pouch

In the late 19th century, thousands of Chinese workers came to Montana to earn money building track for the Northern Pacific Railway. Among them was a man named Ah Hei, who brought this beautiful embroidered pouch with him from China.

Building the railroad line was hard, dangerous work. Laborers cleared land, blasted tunnels through mountains, and laid miles after miles of track to connect the northwestern states. Chinese workers were forced to live in mosquito-infested line camps in very poor conditions and were paid only about a dollar a day—half of what Americans or Canadians were paid.

Far away from their home country, the men cherished mementos from there, like this pouch. It has three pockets and is elaborately decorated with stitched lotus blossoms. Inside it held two good luck coins, a comb, a flint case (the flint used to start fires), and a letter from home written by Ah Hei's brother, Hao Hsing. The letter begged for him to come home, saying "just make enough to buy a ticket home so our mother won't have to worry about you."

Many Chinese immigrants who came to America for work planned to return home, but many died while working dangerous jobs, never making it back to their families. Perhaps Ah Hei was one of them. This pouch now serves as a reminder of the hardworking Chinese people who often gave their lives building the U.S. railroad system.

For more on the Northern Pacific Railway, see page 76.

MAKE A WISH POUCH

First, trace or make a copy of the patterns to the right, then trace on felt and cut out. Apply glue to the back around edges under fold line, then attach the front piece.

Now you are ready to decorate the front section. Use glitter, gems, sequins—anything you want! Glue on a very small piece of Velcro™ to the front and to the inside of the front flap. Once that's dry, close and decorate the front flap.

Write a wish on a small piece of paper and tuck it inside your pouch.

WHAT YOU'LL NEED:

- Felt
- White glue
- Decorating craft supplies: glitter, yarn, sequins, craft gems, pom-poms
- Velcro™
- Small piece of paper
- Pen or pencil

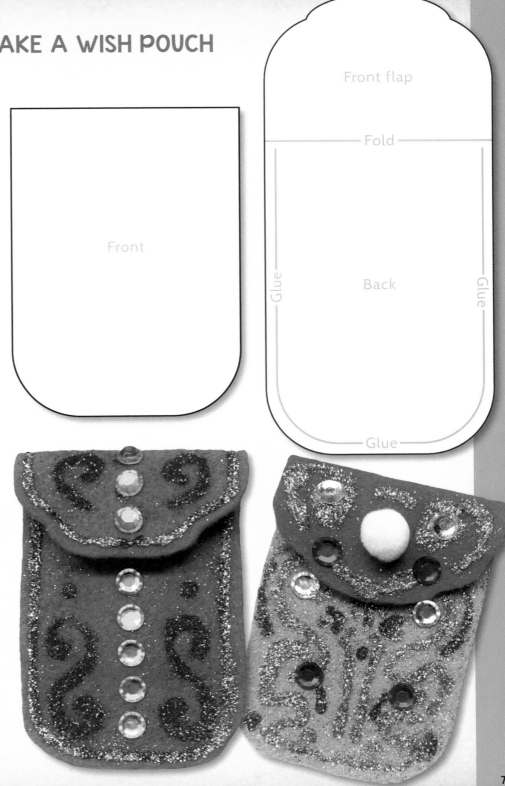

Front flap

Fold

Front

Back

Glue

Glue

Glue

Wish

Fox

Although swift foxes were spiritual animals to Montana's First Peoples, they were unknown to early explorers. On May 31, 1805, near present-day Great Falls, Captain Meriwether Lewis wrote in his journal about the unfamiliar animal: "I saw near those bluffs the most beautifull fox that I ever beheld, the colours appeared to me to be a fine orrange yellow, white and black." But by 1918, the once plentiful swift fox had been exterminated from the short-grass prairies that were once their home, and fifty years later, they were believed to be extinct in Montana.

In the mid-1990s, ten Great Plains states formed the Swift Fox Conservation Team to save the species. In Montana, swift foxes were successfully reintroduced to the Blackfeet Reservation, and then later to the Fort Peck Reservation. Today, swift foxes are once again at home on Montana's prairies.

This sculpture *Swift Fox* was created by Blackfeet artist Jay Polite Laber. His choice of materials may be surprising at first—until you know how deeply he was affected by a 1964 flood that wiped out homes on the reservation and killed many tribal members. Years later, Laber was inspired to pay tribute to the tragedy by using pieces of ruined cars that had washed up along the riverbanks. With these, he created majestic artwork, like the iconic, larger-than-life warriors on horseback that now greet visitors entering the Blackfeet Reservation. And in honor of a species his reservation helped bring back from extinction, he similarly created this incredible swift fox from "junk."

ASSEMBLE YOUR OWN RECYCLED SCULPTURE

WHAT YOU'LL NEED:

- Recyclable materials like the items used in these sculptures: plastic bottles and pump, frozen-food steamer baskets, twist ties, buttons, magazine pages, newspaper, dried-out pens, pieces of plastic, cotton swabs, straw, bottle cap
- Crafting supplies: paint, brushes, glitter, scissors, white glue, low-heat glue gun and sticks, tape

Make a sculpture out of recyclable materials! Start by collecting a bunch of unused objects, like those in the box to the left and milk and egg cartons, popsicle sticks and chopsticks, lids and caps, cardboard boxes and tubes, packing peanuts and bubble wrap, tin and aluminum cans, old clothing, rubber bands, corks, and toothpicks.

Next, think about what you can make from your objects. Can you make a rocket out of a plastic bottle or paper towel roll? A bug or turtle out of an egg carton? A robot out of tin cans or small containers? A boat out of a milk carton? Or a castle out of cardboard boxes? Will your sculpture be just for fun and to look at, or will it have a new use, like the butterfly below that also holds paintbrushes? Use your imagination and have fun!

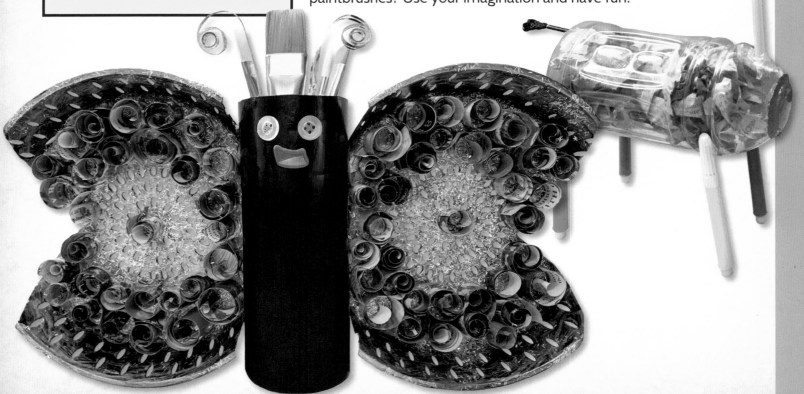

Shoe

Montana was the first state in the nation to elect a woman to a federal office and was also one of the first states to grant women the right to vote. So it's not surprising that Montana has also been home to strong women like Jeannette Rankin.

Jeannette studied biology at the University of Montana in Missoula, her hometown. After graduating in 1902, she traveled to Boston, where she saw poor people living in terrible conditions. Wanting to help people, she became a social worker and teacher. In 1910, she attended the University of Washington, where she got involved in the women's suffrage movement, fighting for women's right to vote. She brought that fight back with her to Montana in 1914—the same year women won the right to vote in her home state. In 1916, Montanans elected her as the first woman to serve in the U.S. House of Representatives. Rankin was a strong advocate for equality, social justice, and peace. She told her fellow members of the House, "I will stand by my country but I will not vote for war," voting against America's involvement in both the First and Second World Wars. Later in life, Rankin continued to work for peace and led an anti-war group protesting the Vietnam War.

In her personal life, she loved stylish clothes and shoes. This is one of the shoes she is shown wearing in her statue in the National Statuary Hall in Washington, D.C. (a second casting of the statue is also in the Montana State Capitol). This gold brocade shoe serves as reminder of the amazing woman who filled it.

Miss Jeannette Rankin

DRAW A PICTURE OF A WOMAN YOU ADMIRE

Famous White Bison

Probably the most famous animal in Montana, "Big Medicine" was an extremely rare white bison that lived his whole life on the National Bison Range. Montana historian Dave Walter noted, "Most Indian bands celebrated the white buffalo as a blessing. . . . The huntsman who killed a white buffalo brought honor not only to himself, but also his family and his entire band."

Born on May 3, 1933, Big Medicine was first named "Whitey" by the Bison Range staff, but then he became known as Big Medicine as his fame grew not only in Montana but across the nation due to his importance to Native peoples. These were the worst years of the Depression, and Walter said, "The symbolism of the remarkable birth was lost on neither native nor Euro American Montanans. . . . The idea of this majestic white animal—whether spiritual icon or remarkable rarity—captured the imagination of a nation struggling to survive a collapsed national economy."

Before the mid-19th century, tens of millions of bison roamed North America. Bison played a central role in the lives of Plains Indians, providing food, shelter, clothing, blankets, tools, and spiritual inspiration. By the late 1800s, only about 1,000 bison remained. Fearing they would become extinct, conservationists founded the American Bison Society in 1905, dedicated to "the permanent preservation and increase of the American Bison." President Theodore Roosevelt urged Congress to purchase land where "a representative herd of bison" could live "to ensure the preservation of the species." The National Bison Range was designated and established on Montana's Flathead Indian Reservation. It started with just thirty-four bison.

The average bison lives about twenty years, but Big Medicine lived to be twenty-six. Because he was so unique, he received a special diet and extra care. As a *Great Falls Tribune* reporter noted in 1959, "He is one of the most photographed animals in the world. People seem to sense an air of mystery about him and gaze in awe at his shining white coat and his crown of dark brown hair. 'Big Medicine,' an appropriate name for a magnificent animal."

Bison String Art

To make your bison pattern, photocopy the drawing on the right at 200%, or larger if you prefer. Paint or stain a piece of wood that is slightly larger than your pattern. If you copied the drawing at 200%, you can use a 5" x 7" piece of wood.

Tape your pattern to your piece of wood and draw dots for your nails along the outline of the bison. Next, lightly hammer a nail in each dot through the paper and into the wood. Once all your nails are in, tear the paper away.

Now you are ready to add your string. Starting at the end of the bison's tail, tie a knot to secure your string, leaving a little extra to tie with when you are finished. Wrap your string around the nails, first going around the outside shape of your bison. When you change direction, wind your string around the nail to secure it and keep the string tight. Next, fill in your bison by criss-crossing your string from nail to nail. It doesn't have to be a certain way. Just keep going until you fill in the shape and then tie your string at the tail when you are finished. If you like, add a tassel to the tail—wrap string around two fingers five times, tie one end of the loop, and cut the other.

WHAT YOU'LL NEED:

- Photocopy of bison
- Black pen
- Piece of wood
  (5" x 7" or larger)
- Tape
- Small nails
- Hammer
- String or embroidery floss

13

Trade Beads

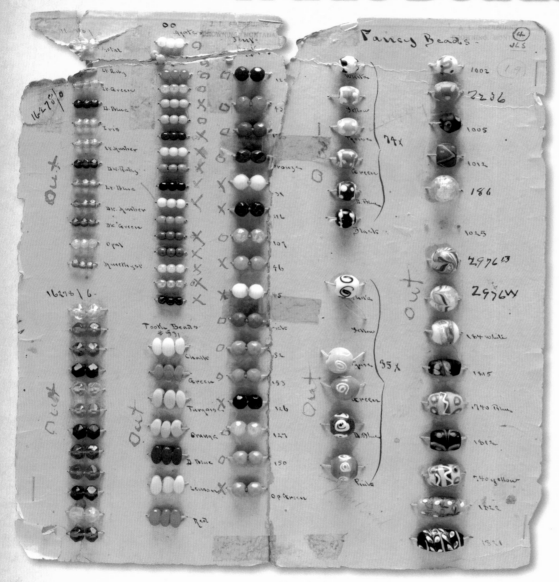

Since before recorded time, Montana's First Peoples have made ornaments to decorate their clothing and other possessions. They used natural materials such as bone, teeth, porcupine quills, wood, and stone.

In the 1600s, European explorers and fur traders introduced glass beads to North America. By the 1820s, Europeans brought their beads to trading posts throughout the West. They were small and easy to transport. Glass was previously unknown to the indigenous peoples, but soon the beads became a prized trade item, replacing traditional ornaments in their decorative designs.

Sample cards were used to show customers the variety of beads a trader had in stock. This card, from about 1910, came from Sherburne Mercantile in Browning, which operated on the Blackfeet Reservation from 1896 to 1942.

With the wide availability of glass beads, beadwork became a favorite form of artwork for the Plains Indians. They are still known for their spectacular beadwork today.

Make a Paper Bead Necklace

To make paper beads for your necklace, you'll need old magazines or wrapping paper. If you are using magazines, tear out pages that are brightly colored. Then trace a triangle pattern onto the pages so all your beads will be about the same size and cut them out. (If you use the pattern to the right, copy it at 250%.) Cut straws into pieces that are larger than the wide end of your triangles and set aside.

Now you are ready to make your beads. With the back side of your triangle facing up, wrap it around a straw once, starting from the wide end. Apply glue or Mod Podge™ to the rest of the triangle's back side, then tightly wrap it around the straw until the pointy end is glued down. Set aside to dry. If you want a shiny coat, apply gloss Mod Podge™ to the outside of your beads. When they have dried, remove the straws and string the beads together as a necklace to wear or to give as a gift.

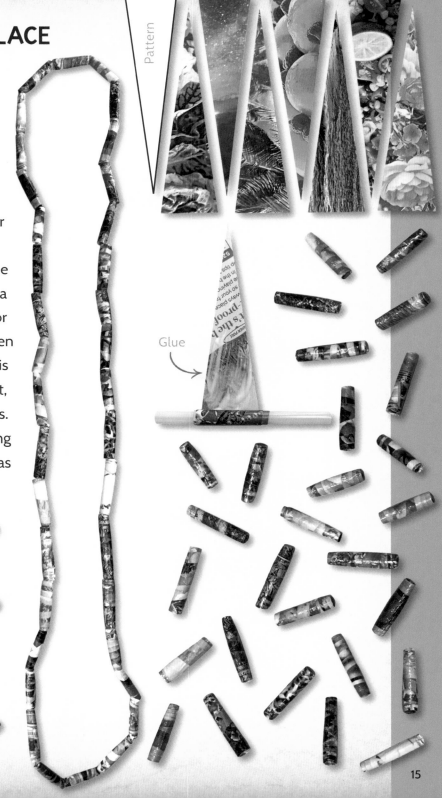

Pattern

Glue

WHAT YOU'LL NEED:

- Magazines or wrapping paper
- Scissors
- Straws
- White glue or Mod Podge™
- String

Anticipating our country's 200th birthday in 1976, the Montana Bicentennial Administration declared the anniversary a "once-in-a-century opportunity to make a better America." By June 1975, Montanans had proposed almost 1,500 bicentennial projects—the third most in the country.

Montanans celebrated in many ways, making bicentennial logos in flower beds, fixing up local museums, writing county history books, and traveling to Billings to see the American Freedom Train that crossed the country in 1975–1976 with twenty-two cars of history exhibits.

One of Montana's bicentennial projects was this mural by Missoula artist James Todd titled *Montana—A Buried History.* Todd, a professor at the University of Montana and a labor activist, said the painting was not only about the Treasure State's history of labor but also about "our Native Americans whose culture was destroyed as a price for the industrialization of Montana."

The top of the painting shows a realistic, modern landscape, while the lower two-thirds show a variety of people and events important to Montana history, such as Lewis and Clark, Charlie Russell, Jeannette Rankin, fur traders, gold miners, family farmers, railroad workers, and tribal warriors of the Battle of Greasy Grass (the Little Bighorn).

DRAW A PICTURE THAT TELLS A STORY

Cookbook

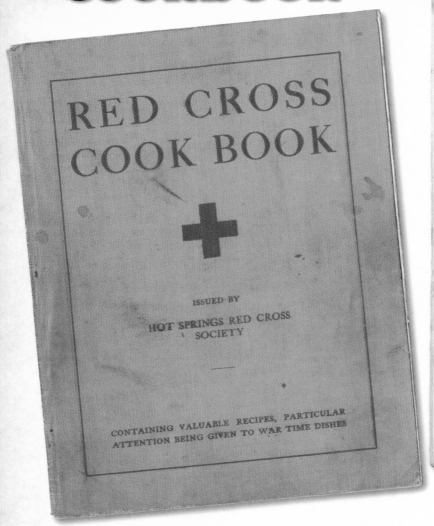

APPLE SAUCE CAKE.

2½ cups hot apple sauce, unseasoned, 2 cups sugar, ½ cup Vegeto
1 tps. each cinnamon, cloves, allspice and salt, 1 lb. raisins chopped,
cup nut meats chopped up, 4 level tps. soda, Ravalli flour and Rava
rolled oats equal parts to make a very stiff batter.

Mrs. Frank Anderson, Hot Springs, Mont.

DEVIL'S FOOD.

By adding 1 square of chocolate to the above recipe and leaving o
all spices except the cloves and adding vanilla a very good devil's fo
will result. If baked in layers just put together with a raisin, fig a
date filling.

Mrs. J. B. McGurk, Missoula, Mont.

GOOD COFFEE CAKE.

2 tbs. fat substitute, pinch of salt, ¼ cup brown sugar, ½ cup molass
1 egg, ½ cup milk; if sour milk add ¼ tps. soda. Put this mixture in
mixing bowl and beat thoroughly with egg beater. 1 heaping tps. ba
ing powder added to enough barley flour to make a very stiff batt
Pour into well greased pan, let stand 10 or 15 minutes and bake
moderate oven. Raisins, currants, chopped dates or figs may be add
if wished.

Mrs. J. B. McGurk, Missoula, Mont.

BLACKBERRY JAM CAKE.

1 cup light brown sugar, ½ cup butter, 2 cups flour, 1 cup blackber
jam, 4 eggs, save 2 whites for icing, 3 tbs. sour cream, 1 tps. soda, 2 t
cinnamon, 1 tps. nutmeg. Cream butter and sugar together and th
put in ingredients, in order given. Cover with white mountain icing.

Mrs. N. W. Ball, Hot Springs, Mont.

This is an excellent recipe, and although it has never been made wi
substitutes, it undoubtedly can be during the war by using some butt
substitute, also by using part substitute for part of flour.

ROLLED OATS COFFEE CAKE.

2½ cups rolled oats (Ravalli), 4 tps. baking powder, ¼ cup suga
½ tps. salt, 1 cup milk, ¼ cup shortening, 1 egg beaten, 2/3 cup raisi
Put rolled oats through food chopper, melt fat, bake for 30 minutes.

Miss Mary Hyre, Columbia City, Indiana.

CREAM PUFFS.

1 cup boiling water, ½ cup butter, boil and stir in 1 cup of flo
when cool add three unbeaten eggs, beat well and drop with tablespo
on greased pan and bake in quick oven 45 minutes. Makes 1 doze
When cool split open and fill with the following made cream or wi
whipped cream: 2 cups milk, ½ cup sugar, 1 egg, 2tbs. cornstarch, s
hot milk into other ingredients, when cool flavor and fill puffs.

Mrs. Grace Kern, Camas, Mont.

—44—

During World War I, women's groups published community cookbooks to raise money and demonstrate "Hooverizing." The term started in 1917 shortly after the United States entered the war, when Herbert Hoover was made head of the U.S. Food Administration. He called on homemakers to do their patriotic duty by conserving food supplies during the war.

WWI cookbooks, like this *Red Cross Cook Book* published in 1918 by the Hot Springs Red Cross Society, featured rationing recipes with "particular attention being given to war time dishes." Dedicated "to our boys on land and sea," this cookbook is a reminder of Montana women's patriotism.

SPONGE CAKE.

1 cup sugar, 1 cup flour, 2 eggs in cup, fill with sweet milk or part cream, 2 tps. baking powder, pinch salt. Bake in moderate oven.

Mrs. Scott Marques, Camas, Mont.

ONE EGG CAKE.

Cream 1 cup sugar with ½ cup butter substitute, add 1 beaten egg, 1 cup sweet milk, 2 cups flour (part substitute), 2 tps. baking powder, mix well and bake in hot oven.

Miss Myrtle B. Irwin, Hot Springs, Mont.

RED CROSS TEA COOKIES.

1 cup sugar, 1 cup minced walnuts, 1 cup cocoanut, 3 cups cornflakes, whites of 4 eggs beaten to an extra stiff froth. Mix dry ingredients together and add eggs, mix well and bake on wax paper in drop cookie style in a slow oven.

Mrs. C. M. Willis, Hot Springs, Mont.

POTATO FLOUR CAKE.

4 eggs beaten separately with a little salt, add ½ glass of sugar to whites and ½ glass to yolk, beat together 3 minutes, sift level tps. baking powder in ½ glass potato flour, add to eggs and sugar, put in 2 layer pans, drop pans to table 2 or 3 times and bake in slow oven. Frost with orange juice and powdered sugar.

Miss Myrtle B. Irwin, Hot Springs, Mont.

GOOD ROLLED OATS CAKE.

Put in mixing bowl ½ cup sugar, 1 egg well beaten, add ¾ cup sour milk, 1 cup raisins cut into small pieces, ¼ tps. salt, 1 tps. cinnamon, 1½ cups rolled oats put through little food chopper, then add ½ cup white flour and ¾ tps. soda, dissolved in little hot water.

Mrs. Gus Marquardt, Hot Springs, Mont.

NUT CAKE.

2 cups of white sugar, 1 cup of butter, yolks of 4 eggs, 1 cup of cold water, 3 cups of flour, 2 tps of baking powder, whites of four eggs, 2 cups chopped nuts, a little salt. Season with vanilla.

Mrs. Ella Baker, Kalispell, Mont.

One can use substitutes with these recipes with good results.

DEVIL'S CAKE.

1 large cup sugar, 1 large cup sweet milk, 1 large cup flour, 2 eggs, 1 cake Baker's chocolate, butter size egg, 1 level tps. soda. Melt butter and chocolate on stove, when melted remove and add sugar, stir well, eggs, milk and soda and flour sifted together. This will make 3 layers, medium size; any filling is nice with it; excellent with whipped cream.

Mrs. Adam J. Whiston, Hot Springs, Mont.

—45—

BAKE

Bake a vintage recipe from the *Red Cross Cook Book!* Recipes from the WWI era not only rationed ingredients, they were more vague than recipes today. They often used unfamiliar ingredients and measurements and lacked specific baking temperatures and times. Why? Because making meals for their family took most of a homemaker's day, they already knew cooking techniques, so the recipes showcased new ideas rather than basic instructions.

WHAT IS THAT?

- Vegetole = Cooking fat or oil
- Sweet milk = whole milk
- 1 glass = 1 cup
- Butter size egg = ¼ cup butter
- Slow oven = 300 degrees
- Moderate oven = 350 degrees
- Quick oven = 375 to 400 degrees
- Hot oven = 400 to 425 degrees

TIP: When no oven temperature is listed, bake at 350 degrees. For cakes, insert a toothpick into the center. If it comes out clean, the cake is done.

Rodeo Sculpture

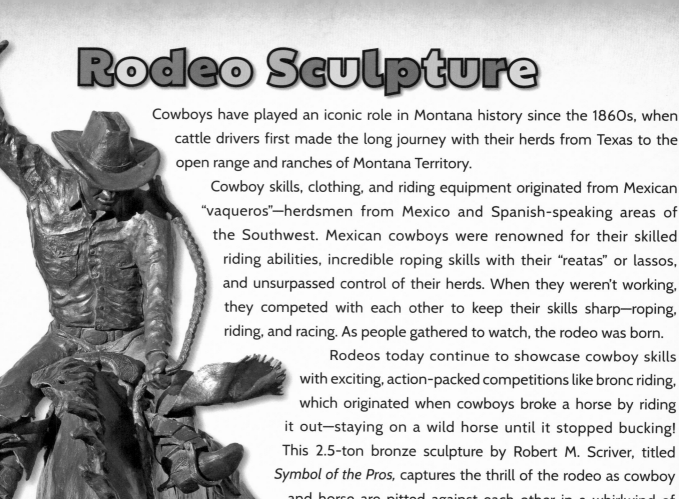

Cowboys have played an iconic role in Montana history since the 1860s, when cattle drivers first made the long journey with their herds from Texas to the open range and ranches of Montana Territory.

Cowboy skills, clothing, and riding equipment originated from Mexican "vaqueros"—herdsmen from Mexico and Spanish-speaking areas of the Southwest. Mexican cowboys were renowned for their skilled riding abilities, incredible roping skills with their "reatas" or lassos, and unsurpassed control of their herds. When they weren't working, they competed with each other to keep their skills sharp—roping, riding, and racing. As people gathered to watch, the rodeo was born.

Rodeos today continue to showcase cowboy skills with exciting, action-packed competitions like bronc riding, which originated when cowboys broke a horse by riding it out—staying on a wild horse until it stopped bucking! This 2.5-ton bronze sculpture by Robert M. Scriver, titled *Symbol of the Pros,* captures the thrill of the rodeo as cowboy and horse are pitted against each other in a whirlwind of action. Scriver was born on the Blackfeet Reservation and worked at his studio in Browning. Inspired by the geography, people, and animals in the Glacier Park area—and the romance of the Wild West—he is considered one of the nation's most celebrated sculptors of Western life. When Scriver died in 1999, art museums across North America wanted his collection. But his wife, Lorraine, wanting his masterpieces to stay with the people of Montana, donated 3,000 pieces to the Montana Historical Society.

Make a Rodeo Game

Make your own horses for a rodeo game. Your horses can be any colors you want!

1. To make the body, fold one pipe cleaner in half and twist the halves together to make a head and neck.

2. Cut your second pipe cleaner in half for two sets of legs. For each, make a circle and then fold it to make a "V" shape.

3. Twist the body pipe cleaners to attach the first set of legs around the front of the body.

4. Next, attach the second set of legs a little farther down the body, then twist the rest of the two pipe cleaner halves to form what looks like a long tail.

5. Wrap the tail back around the body up toward the head.

6. Cut two small pieces from your third pipe cleaner, preferably in another color, and form into a curvy shape for the mane and tail.

7. Glue the mane and tail on your horse.

8. Tie a "lasso" out of twine.

After you make several horses and lassos, you are ready to play rodeo! With your friends or family, take turns throwing the lassos to see who can catch the most horses!

Elk Tooth Dress

This elk-tooth dress was made sometime between 1830 and 1860. Indian agent Major Rufus A. Allen acquired the dress during his survey of the Blackfeet Indian Reservation in the 1880s.

The dress is fifty-four inches long and made from two tanned hides, possibly from bighorn sheep. It was originally decorated with 192 elk "eye teeth," which were probably collected over several years. (Elk eye teeth are also called elk ivory. They are upper teeth believed to be the remnants of tusks from their prehistoric ancestors.) Elk teeth were typically used for women's and girls' clothing—and since a single dress with 50 to 300 of these teeth could be traded for as much as two horses, the large amount of teeth on this dress tells us that the wearer was an important person.

Elk-teeth decorations date back to the Mandan who lived on the lower Missouri River in the 14th century. The custom then spread to other tribes, including the Blackfeet, by 1800.

In the second half of the 19th century, clothing began to change. Traders brought wool cloth, which started replacing hides for clothing material. At the time, Indian reservations were being established and fewer large game animals were available, which made it difficult to collect large quantities of elk teeth. Even so, traditional women's dresses for tribal ceremonies are still decorated with both real and imitation elk teeth today.

Major Allen's collection was described as "probably the most complete and interesting collection that has ever been gathered to illustrate the dress, ornaments, implements, and weapons of any single tribe of Indians within this state." The *Helena Daily Independent* declared, "It is desirable that . . . this collection, which is so closely identified with the beginnings of Montana history, be kept within the state for the present and future benefit of the people." Copper King William A. Clark made that happen when he purchased Allen's collection in its entirety and donated it to the Montana Historical Society.

DESIGN AND DECORATE CLOTHES YOU WOULD LIKE TO WEAR

Bicycle

Chainless bicycles, like this one that belonged to the Reverend Edwin M. Ellis, were popular during the 1890s. Without a chain to get clogged with mud or tangled with weeds, it served the reverend well on the rough dirt roads he traveled while serving the Presbyterian Church in Montana.

Ellis came to the Bitterroot Valley in 1884 at the request of Dr. Sheldon Jackson, superintendent of Presbyterian missions in the western part of the state. Headquartered in Stevensville, Ellis first traveled on horseback to preach wherever he could, from schoolhouses to people's living rooms. By the 1890s, Presbyterianism was thriving in the area. In an effort to reach more children, the reverend was put in charge of supervising the many Sunday schools spread out across the state. He moved to Helena for access to the railroad, which helped him to travel quickly, but many remote places could not be reached by train, or even stagecoach, so he used this bicycle.

Historical objects tell many stories, quite a few of them unexpected. This beat-up chainless bicycle looks ordinary, but it tells the story of an extraordinary man so dedicated to what he believed in that he was willing to bike more than 36,000 miles across Montana to go wherever he was needed.

FOLLOW THE CHALK PATH

For your path, first make a thick, curvy line with your chalk going down the sidewalk. Decorate around the path with flowers or other objects that players should not ride or step on.

When you are finished with your path and obstacles to avoid, ride your bike on the line, being careful not to get off your chalk path until the finish line.

If you are doing the path activity with family or friends who don't have a bike, take turns walking on the path very fast without falling off. See who can walk the path the fastest!

If you want to make it even more challenging, try hopping on one foot, or walking backwards down the path. What else can you do with your chalk path?

FUN FACT: Some say ants will not cross a chalk path (although it probably only works for a short time).

WHAT YOU'LL NEED:

- A long sidewalk
- Sidewalk chalk

Horse Ornament

In the early 1700s, horses replaced dogs as the new beast of burden for Montana's tribes. They allowed people to travel faster and farther. Pend d'Oreille, inland Salish, and Kootenai tribes acquired horses from the Nez Perce and Shoshone, who were successfully breeding horses. By the late 1700s, Plains and Plateau peoples had become master horsemen. They trained their horses for war, bison hunting, and travel. By the 1800s, horses were considered essential to survival and well-being. With horses, tribes on the west side of the Rocky Mountains could hunt bison twice a year on the eastern plains. Horses made trade possible with faraway tribes, like the Crow. Horses also brought them closer to their enemies. Young warriors earned honor by capturing these valuable animals from other tribes.

The tradition of outfitting horses with elaborate decorations for special occasions represented not only the prestige of the rider but also the essential role of horses in Native cultures. The tradition is still practiced today at parades, celebrations, and powwows.

This otter-pelt ornament would have been displayed behind the saddle with a matching ornament on the other side. It was made by Elizabeth Ashley, a descendant of English and French fur traders and a member of the Upper Pend d'Oreille (Q'lispé) Tribe of the Flathead Reservation. Intermarriage was common between European traders and Northwest indigenous peoples. During the 1800s, the extensive Ashley family married into the Salish, Pend d'Oreille, Kootenai, and Spokane tribes.

Today, as in the past, horses are given as honored gifts for special occasions, such as naming ceremonies and weddings. At cultural events, like the Arlee Powwow and Crow Fair, horses are elaborately decorated in beaded bridles, ornate saddles, colorful saddle blankets, and other ornaments, then paraded in glory befitting their enduring significance to Montana's Native peoples.

Make a Horse Ornament

Instead of making an ornament for a horse, let's make a horse-inspired ornament! To prepare, tear newspaper into strips about 1" x 2". It's okay if they are a little larger or smaller. Blow up a balloon to the size you want your ornament. Then, make a paste by mixing flour and water in a bowl. You want it to be a little thin, like cake batter, and without lumps.

Now you are ready to make a papier-mâché ornament! Put your balloon in a bowl to hold it while working. Dip each piece of newspaper in the paste and apply it to your balloon, smoothing lumps and extra paste with your fingers. Cover your entire balloon with one thin layer. Tie a string to the top of the balloon and hang somewhere to dry.

Once dry, apply a second coat of papier-mâché. When the second layer is dry, you can pop your balloon and remove it from the shell.

Paint and decorate your ornament with a horse theme. When you are finished, tie a toothpick to a string or thin wire. Insert the toothpick into the hole. When it turns horizontal, it will stay in for hanging.

WHAT YOU'LL NEED:

- Newspaper
- One cup flour
- One cup water
- Craft supplies for decorating, including paint, tissue paper, pipe cleaners, beads, etc.
- String or wire for hanging
- Toothpick

Montana's 1st Map

With the 1864 gold rush in Bannack and Virginia City, thousands of people started coming to Montana hoping to strike it rich. At the time, Montana was part of Idaho Territory, but with the growing population, Congress divided the region into two separate territories. At the first Montana Territorial Legislature held on December 17, 1864, delegates decided that they needed a map. Charles Bagg on the Committee on Mines and Minerals—a group that promoted gold mining in Montana—hired Captain Walter W. DeLacy to produce this map in just fifteen days. It shows the nine original counties, plus mountains, waterways, and mining districts. As the first map of Montana, it was an important reference for many years for miners, ranchers, farmers, and people investing in land. Today it still serves as an important reference for historians, researchers, novelists, and filmmakers as a map of Montana's past.

DRAW A MAP OF YOUR NEIGHBORHOOD, YARD, OR HOUSE

Printing Press

When new towns started springing up in the Montana Territory in the 1860s, so did local newspapers. The first to be printed on a regular basis was *The Montana Post*, published weekly from 1864 to 1869. It was 21" x 31" and had six columns. The newspaper was printed on this Lowe Press No. 2, first in Virginia City, and then in Helena after March 1868. It featured stories about frontier vigilantes who took the law into their own hands, local and post-Civil War politics, business in the new territory, and of course, the gold rush.

The Lowe Press No. 2 was invented by Samuel W. Lowe of Philadelphia and patented in 1856. Letterpresses like this one use relief printing of individual raised letter blocks put together in a bed to spell words on the printing plate. After the letter blocks are all set to make a story, the plate is inked and paper is pressed to it by a roller, transferring the plate's text to the paper. The Lowe Press No. 2 was unusual in that it had a cone-shaped roller instead of a cylindrical one. Advertised as easy to use, small, and portable, its slogan was "Every Man His Own Printer!" This press made printing available not only to newspapers but also to business owners, clergymen, lawyers, and the military during and after the Civil War.

Dozens of newspapers in Montana were also published in German, Swedish, Serbian, Croatian, and other languages. Farmers, ranchers, miners, socialists, and labor unions printed special-interest newspapers as well. Printing presses spread the sharing of knowledge and stories, so they were important to the developing frontier. Today, the Montana Historical Society holds 95 percent of all the newspapers ever published in the Treasure State, providing a record of daily life, culture, and politics from 1864 to the present.

Make Prints at Home

Block printing is a centuries-old relief printing process, but instead of individual letters, whole pages with words and pictures are carved into the wooden printing plate. The printer applies ink to the surface and uses pressure to transfer the image to paper. You can make an easy block print with foam plates using washed Styrofoam™ meat trays left over from the grocery store (that are free!) or foam sheets from a craft store. Start by cutting your Styrofoam™ into a rectangular plate. Cut pieces of paper a little larger than your printing plate and set aside.

Next, draw a design on your foam plate by pressing a pencil or pen firmly into the soft Styrofoam™. The design you draw will print in white against whatever color ink or paint you apply to the plate.

Pour paint or squeeze printing ink onto a paper plate or piece of cardboard. Roll the brayer or dab your foam brush in the paint or ink. Apply an even layer of color to your Styrofoam™ printing plate. Be careful it doesn't seep into the grooves of your design.

Lay a piece of paper on your printing plate. Careful not to move it, gently rub the top of your paper with your hands or the back of a spoon. Lift your paper and enjoy your print!

TIP: Your print will be in reverse from your drawing, so if you write anything, you must write it backwards.

WHAT YOU'LL NEED:

- Styrofoam™ trays or sheets
- Pencil or pen
- Craft paint or water-based printing ink
- Brayer (printmaking rubber roller) or wide foam brush
- Water media paper

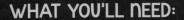

Montana Seal

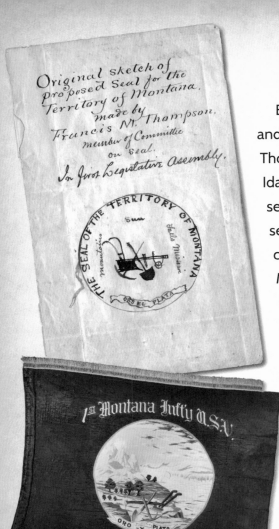

Every state in the nation has an official seal with symbols of its history, people, and geography. Montana's seal started with this sketch on the left by Francis M. Thompson, who came to the area during the gold rush in 1862 when it was still Idaho Territory. When Montana became its own territory in 1864, Thompson served on the Montana Territorial Council and was in charge of designing a seal. In 1865, Governor Sidney Edgerton made Thompson's seal official. In the center it has a farmer's plow and miner's pick and shovel to represent Montana's early non-native residents. On the bottom is a banner with the motto *"Oro y Plata,"* which means "Gold and Silver" in Spanish. And on the left it says "Mountains," the top center "Sun," and the right "Falls Missouri" to represent Montana's scenic beauty.

In 1889, Montana was made a state, and a few years later Governor John E. Rickards decided it needed a new state seal. Based on the original sketch, the new seal used images for the mountains and Great Falls, and the word "territory" was replaced with "state."

In 1895, Colonel Harry Kessler, commander of the Montana National Guard, had this blue flag made with the seal as a traveling trophy. It was then used by the First Montana Volunteers during the Spanish-American War. In 1905, it became the official state flag with the addition of the state's name above the seal.

Some people were upset that the seal's motto was in Spanish when the Spanish-American War had cost so many soldiers' lives, and that the motto was more concerned with material wealth—gold and silver—than higher morals like justice and liberty. But in spite of these concerns, the seal remains today much as it started with Thompson's sketch celebrating Montana's mineral and agricultural wealth and its beautiful landscapes beneath a big sky.

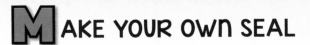AKE YOUR OWN SEAL

Make a family or friendship seal! Think of symbols for the people and pets in your life—what you like to do together and what makes them special. Choose your colors and a motto that captures the spirit of your group.

Hunters

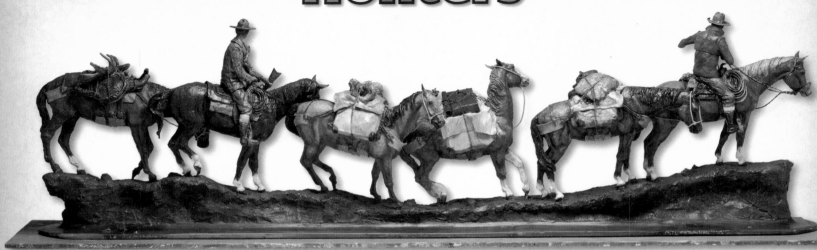

This clay sculpture by Earl E. Heikka shows a lead horseman guiding a five-horse pack string on a hunting trip. Titled *Trophy Hunters,* it is inspired by the artist's real-life experiences working as a guide with his favorite brother, Mike, for a well-known hunting and fishing outfitter, the K Bar L Ranch, based northwest of Augusta, near the Bob Marshall Wilderness.

Earl was always good with the details. Emil Klick, who helped establish the K Bar L Ranch in 1927, said Earl "noticed things about the animals, how they looked and how they were packed—things most kids his age would never pay any attention to, and few older folks would either." He captured that accurate attention to detail in this sculpture with the hunters' clothing, their weapons, and the pack horses' loads.

Earl first showed his talent for sculpting when modeling animals from mud for his young nephews. While working as a taxidermist in Great Falls, he grew famous as an artist and he soon had commissions to create art for people, invitations to national shows, and his own sculpture exhibit in Los Angeles.

Earl Heikka died in 1941 at the young age of thirty-one, but during his life he produced more than 200 sculptures of Montana life with cowboys, miners, and hunters. He had a unique method of working with clay that produced pieces that rarely if ever cracked—a drying process that master artists still don't fully understand and can only be attributed to his background in taxidermy.

Although he had no formal training, Earl Heikka's work is recognized as some of the best sculpture representing the American West today.

Make a paper horse with moving legs

To make your horse with moving legs, photocopy the pattern to the right at 200%. Color your horse's legs and body BEFORE cutting them out. When you do cut out the pieces, keep track of the position of the legs. Punch holes as shown.

To assemble your horse, put the back foreleg down first, then the horse's chest over it, then the top foreleg, and align all the holes. Insert a brad fastener through the holes and flatten the two prongs on the back. Do the same for the hind legs on your horse's thigh.

Now, cut pieces of yarn for your horse's mane and tail and glue on. Let dry.

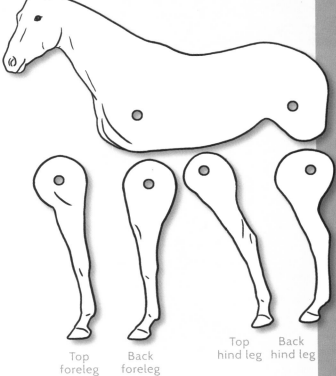

Top foreleg   Back foreleg   Top hind leg   Back hind leg

WHAT YOU'LL NEED:

- Photocopy of horse
- Crayons or colored pencils
- Scissors
- Hole punch
- Brad fasteners
- Yarn
- White glue

Grotesque

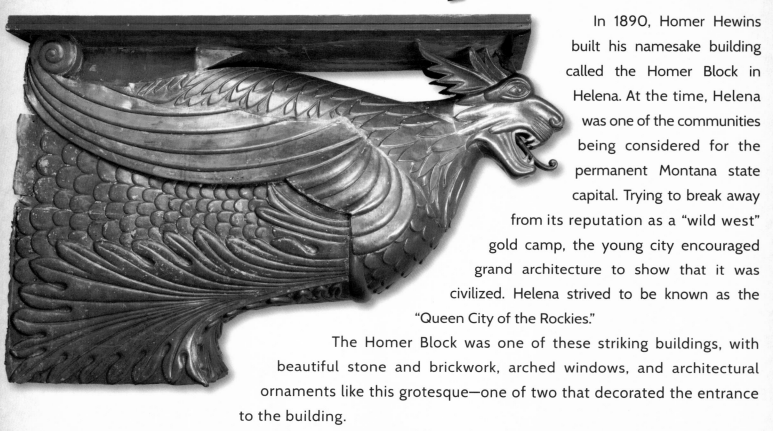

In 1890, Homer Hewins built his namesake building called the Homer Block in Helena. At the time, Helena was one of the communities being considered for the permanent Montana state capital. Trying to break away from its reputation as a "wild west" gold camp, the young city encouraged grand architecture to show that it was civilized. Helena strived to be known as the "Queen City of the Rockies."

The Homer Block was one of these striking buildings, with beautiful stone and brickwork, arched windows, and architectural ornaments like this grotesque—one of two that decorated the entrance to the building.

In modern times, the word "grotesque" is often used to describe something ugly or disgusting, like a Halloween mask. But architectural grotesques, also called chimeras, are fantastical creatures often created with a mix of different animals, humans, dragons, and demons. They are commonly confused with gargoyles—both unnatural-looking creatures that can be scary to frighten off evil spirits to protect churches and homes. But grotesques are purely decorative, and gargoyles also serve as water spouts, directing rain water through their mouths so it doesn't run down the building, damaging the stone and mortar.

The Homer Block's twin grotesques were fashioned after ancient mythical creatures that once guarded temples and other buildings. When the Homer Block was demolished in 1971, Glen Wilson bought the two grotesques. His aunt, who had managed a shop in the building, used to repaint the grotesques' features every year, but Glen stripped the paint off one and discovered the original beautiful copper color.

Sculpt Your Own Grotesque

Make your own grotesque out of air-dry clay to guard your room or house. First, make a base from the clay for your sculpture to sit on, then form your sculpture. Remember, a grotesque can be an unnatural creature created from parts from different animals, humans, or mythological creatures like dragons.

After your sculpture dries (it may take a few days—follow instructions on your clay package), color your grotesque with acrylic paint. It can be gold, copper, silver, or gray if you want it to look like stone or metal. After the paint dries, you can spray it with clear sealant spray—gloss if you want it extra shiny or matte for a stone look.

Create fun patterns with a straw, toothpicks, and a plastic knife!

WHAT YOU'LL NEED:

- Air-dry clay
- Tools to make decorative patterns and textures like toothpicks, a straw, and/or a plastic knife.
- Metallic or gray acrylic paint
- Clear sealant spray (optional)

37

Dog Painting

People were not the only Montanans to serve in war—horses and mules were used to transport men and equipment, and dogs were trained for rescue missions at camps like the War Dog Reception and Training Center at Camp Rimini.

Kenya, the Siberian husky in this painting, was one of about 800 sled dogs stationed at Camp Rimini between 1942 and 1944. Musher Eddie Barbeau brought Kenya with him from Minnesota to be his lead sled dog. Barbeau not only trained dogs and men, he was also in charge of buying dogs from all over the northern United States and Canada to train at the camp for military rescue missions in cold, Arctic climates.

Camp Rimini was in the mountains near Helena. It started as a silver-mining camp, then was a camp for the Civilian Conservation Corps. When the U.S. Army needed a place to train winter rescue dogs and the men who handled them during World War II, Camp Rimini offered existing buildings, access to lots of public land, and perfect training conditions with long, cold winters and deep snow. Soldiers learned how to survive in extreme winter weather; how to care for their dogs; and how to build sleds, dog packs, harnesses, and other supplies.

After their training was complete, the soldier-and-dog teams were sent to strategic locations along the two major Arctic flyways to rescue airmen whose planes crashed in the far north. It's said that they saved around 150 downed airmen and salvaged millions of dollars of equipment during the war!

When you first looked at this dog painting, did you think you would be looking at a U.S. Army hero?

RAW OR PAINT A PET

Draw or paint a picture of your pet—or your dream pet! What makes your pet awesome?

Lithograph

For early Montana children, manufactured toys and games were rare. They had to use their imaginations to create their own fun. And for those who lived at remote homesteads, their siblings, pets, and farm animals served as their playmates. This lithograph, titled *Playing Circus* by Montana artist Fanny Cory Cooney, captures that creative play as the kids put on a circus show with a rooster that is supposed to be an ostrich, the family dog that has been striped to be a tiger, and the baby brother who's forced by the older siblings to be the imprisoned "Wild Man."

Playing Circus was part of a series of Cooney lithographs published in 1904 by Harper & Bros. Each scene was produced in at least two versions, with one accompanied by a descriptive poem. For *Playing Circus,* it read:

> *We're planning for a circus—*
> *It's the nicest kind of play,*
> *We hope that some grown-ups'll come,*
> *'Cause they have got to pay.*
> *The wild-man really howls because he thinks it isn't fun;*
> *And you just better wait until the tight-rope act's begun!*

After graduating from Helena High School, Fanny went to New York City in 1895 to study art and work as an illustrator under the pen name F. Y. Cory. Her career was put on hold when she returned to Montana after the death of her sister. In 1904, she married Fred Cooney and they settled on a remote ranch near the Missouri River, "27 miles from Helena . . . and 3 miles from anything." Fanny was so busy with their children and ranch life that she didn't have time to create her art until the 1920s, when her children had grown. Combining her talent with her observations of her own children, she created comics in three separate newspaper series from 1926 to 1956. Her most popular and longest-running comic was *Sonnysayings,* featuring a curly-headed, five-year-old boy.

Whether she was drawing her comic series or creating lithographs like *Playing Circus,* Fanny Cory Cooney captured the spirit of children, both charming and mischievous.

MAKE A MONOPRINT!

Monoprinting is fun! Instead of making many prints of the same image, you only make one print of each image, and that lets you experiment with different colors, images, textures, and techniques.

To start with, you need a piece of plexiglass for your printing plate. If you don't have one, you can use the bottom of a baking dish. You can apply the paint or ink either of two ways: with a brush or with a roller. You can paint with a paintbrush similar to how you paint on paper (but your image is going to be in reverse).

Or you can apply paint or ink all over your printing plate, either by brush or roller. Then "draw" your image with a cotton swab or your finger, removing the paint for the lines. It's also interesting to experiment with textures by dragging a comb through the paint or pressing something into it like bubble wrap. Have fun! If you don't like it, you can wipe it off and start again. Just make sure you don't take too long or the paint will dry on your plate.

When you are satisfied with your image, you are ready to make a print. Carefully lay down a damp piece of watercolor paper. Without moving the paper, press down firmly all over. Lift your paper and you'll see your print!

WHAT YOU'LL NEED:

- Plexiglass or baking dish
- Paint or printing ink
- Paintbrushes or foam roller
- Water media paper
- Cotton swabs, comb, bubble wrap, etc.

"Bomb"

Unlike most bombs that can hurt and kill people, this very special "bomb" was created to save lives!

During World War II, the U.S. Army's Psychological Warfare Division wanted to distribute many leaflets to enemy soldiers, encouraging them to surrender. James Buckley, who had worked previously as a sheet-metal worker for the Anaconda Copper Mining Company, used his unique skills to develop a "bomb" that could drop 30,000 pieces of printed paper over a fifteen-mile radius!

When Buckley looked back on his invention, he said, "I was flying by my shirt tails." He wasn't trained in aircraft weaponry, so he improvised his device mainly from a fuel tank from a British Spitfire aircraft. A series of bungee cords would release the bomb. "It was so simple," Buckley explained, "but that's why nobody else would have thought of it. If it had been high-tech, I wouldn't have been able to do a thing with it."

The bomb was successfully tested in 1944 and then was used in the war over Germany and Japan. "I think it played a pretty important part," Buckley recalled. "A small part, but an important one."

On May 11, 1946, Buckley was awarded the Bronze Star in a ceremony in Butte for his ingenious invention of the Buckley Bomb. It was responsible for the surrender of thousands of enemy troops, thereby saving the lives of soldiers on both sides.

This is the model Buckley built for his bomb made out of cracker tins. He donated it to the Montana Historical Society in 1997, along with his design plans and his Bronze Star. When asked what he hoped future generations would remember about WWII, Buckley said, "I think they should remember that it happened, and all of the different things that brought it to an end. I am proud that in a small way I was one of so many who helped."

Make a Baking Soda Bomb

A baking soda "bomb" is another kind of bomb that won't hurt you. It's really a cool science experiment about chemical reaction.

When baking soda and vinegar are combined, they break apart and form a new chemical—a gas called carbon dioxide. Trapped in a plastic ziplock bag, the soda and vinegar create bubbles that expand, filling the bag and stretching the plastic until the pressure is too much and it explodes!

First, add vinegar, water, and food coloring to the plastic bag. Add baking soda to the center of a piece of paper towel, then fold it to make an envelope that holds the baking soda inside.

The next part should be done outside or in a kitchen sink or bathtub. With most of the plastic bag closed, drop the envelope of baking soda into the vinegar and water mixture and quickly close the bag. Shake to mix, then put the bag down, stand back, and watch. The chemical reaction happens very quickly, and the gas in the bag will bubble and expand until it **POPS!**

POP!

WHAT YOU'LL NEED:

- Sandwich-size ziplock bag
- $1/2$ cup white vinegar
- $1/2$ cup warm water
- Two drops food coloring
- $1^1/2$ tablespoons baking soda
- 6" x 6" piece of paper towel

Portrait

Butte artist Elizabeth Davey Lochrie was an artist well-known for painting Native American portraits, like this painting of Cecile Black Boy.

Lochrie was born in Deer Lodge and studied at the Pratt Institute in New York, an art school taught by Winold Reiss in Glacier National Park, and Stanford University, where she learned how to paint murals. In 1923, Governor Joseph Dixon commissioned her to paint a series of murals for the children's ward at the Montana State Tuberculosis Sanitarium at Galen.

But her true passion was painting portraits of Montana's Native people. Her friend, Helen Clarke, called her a "historian with a brush" because she included on the back of her paintings information about the people she painted and their culture. "Each Indian I paint," Lochrie wrote, "I see as an individual, not as a racial type, and since most show a strong personality it makes them especially interesting subjects to portray."

Cecile Black Boy—whose name in the Siksika (Blackfoot) language was *Noomohtsiistaapitapi Sstaniiniki* (Tobacco Pod Woman)—was a remarkable person. She collected hundreds of Blackfeet stories for the Montana Writer's Project from 1939–1942. This painting of her not only shows Lochrie's talent as a portrait artist but also honors Cecile Black Boy, who worked to preserve her Blackfeet heritage.

In *Montana: An Artist's Paradise,* Lochrie wrote that people who find "a creative outlet experience a greater joy than the average person."

DRAW A SELF-PORTRAIT

Look in a mirror and draw a picture of yourself.

Heart Monitor

This funny-looking contraption looks like it might play groovy music or an old movie, but it's an early heart monitor invented by Helena native Norman Jefferis "Jeff" Holter and his partner William Glasscock. It revolutionized the study and treatment of heart disease.

From an early age, Jeff was encouraged to pursue his interest in science and technology. After graduating from Carroll College in 1931, Jeff continued his education in physics and chemistry at universities in California, Illinois, Germany, and Oregon.

Holter joined the U.S. Navy in the early 1940s and became a senior physicist, studying the effects of atomic bombs that exploded underwater. He grew to dislike nuclear weapons. After the Navy, he returned to Helena and established the Holter Research Foundation—located first in the back of his parents' hardware store and then in an abandoned train station. The goal of his foundation was to "follow whatever idea appears most likely to lead us to things not previously known." He explained, "We have no idea what we might be working on a year from now. It could be anything from outer space to bird feathers."

Holter and Glasscock first created a prototype for their new kind of heart monitor. There were already big machines that recorded the actions of the heart, but Holter's was unique because it was small enough that it could be carried alongside a patient, recording his or her heartbeat during activity. After a few more prototypes, Holter's heart monitor went into commercial production in 1962.

Even with his success, he was always more interested in science than in making money off of his inventions. He continued to pursue advancements in science and technology, and he and his wife, Joan Treacy Holter, donated money to local institutions, like the Holter Museum of Art in Helena.

Today, current versions of the Holter Heart Monitor are the size of a cell phone and are used around the world.

Make a "Stained-Glass" Heart

Everyone recognizes this 🖤 as a symbol for a heart. Find a picture of a human heart. Do the two hearts look alike or different?

For your stained glass, first draw half a heart symbol on paper for a pattern, then cut out the center, leaving a border about 1" thick. Trace your pattern on a folded piece of construction paper with the fold at the open side of the heart half, then cut it out for your stained-glass frame. Tear off two sheets of wax paper slightly bigger than your heart frame. Next, grate crayons to make piles of different color crayon shavings. Lay down paper towels under your wax paper. Sprinkle crayon shavings all over one piece of wax paper. Cover with the second piece of wax paper and carefully transfer it to an ironing board, picking it up by the paper towels. Cover with more paper towels and, with the help of an adult, run a hot iron over it until the crayon shavings melt. When cool, glue on your heart frame. When dry, trim off excess wax paper. Lastly, draw geometric shapes with a permanent marker to look like stained glass. Punch two holes as shown below and tie with string to hang in a window.

WHAT YOU'LL NEED:

- White paper (for pattern)
- Construction paper
- Scissors
- Crayons
- Potato peeler, grater, or crayon sharpener
- Paper towels
- Wax paper
- Iron
- Glue
- Hole punch
- String

Russell Painting

To represent the Treasure State's Old West past, it's hard to find anything better than the magnificent artwork of Montana's own "Cowboy Artist" Charles M. Russell. He created over 2,000 paintings of cowboys, Indians, wildlife, and landscapes.

Called "the greatest of all Russells," *When the Land Belonged to God* shows the artist at his best—masterfully capturing Montana's past before it was changed forever by miners and farmers. He painted the West that was, with incredibly rendered wildlife in their natural, unspoiled habitat. In this masterpiece, he shows sunrise on the Missouri River a few miles from Fort Benton, as an endless stream of bison crosses the river. The lead group emerges from the water to the unwelcome sight of hungry wolves and bison skeletons.

The painting was commissioned by Helena's famed Montana Club in 1914, then was sold to the state in the mid-1970s. Governor Tom Judge said, "The work of Charlie Russell and a handful of other artists and writers has kept those of us who were not fortunate enough to know the Old West firsthand from forgetting her. . . . His paintings—their color, drama and size—bring home to us forcefully the dreams of independence and reverence for nature which underlie the quality of life we Montanans work hard to nurture and defend."

Color This Charles M. Russell Painting

Break out your colored pencils and color this C. M. Russell painting titled *The Herd Quitter.*

Charlie painted what he loved—the American West. Born near St. Louis, Missouri, in 1864, "Kid" Russell moved to Montana in 1880 and, two years later, became a working cowboy when he was just eighteen years old. He continued to work for different ranches for several years, painting and sketching along the way. In 1894, he gave up cowboying to become a full-time artist.

Loom

Amanda Perälä Kraftenberg and her husband, Fred, immigrated from Lapua, Finland, to Montana in 1899. They homesteaded near Little Belt Creek in the Korpivaara or "Wilderness Hill" community in Cascade County—an area known for its finely crafted log homes of traditional Finnish construction and modern design.

Like other Finns in the area, the Kraftenbergs' home life was a unique blend of Finnish cultural practices and Montana's natural heritage. From 1916 until 1952, Amanda wove a variety of items on this Finnish-style four-harness counterbalance loom. It was built by John "Jack" Veeda out of pine and willow from the nearby Highwood Mountains. The loom was described by Montana weaver Milly Dover, who grew up in Belt, as "Wonderful! Workable!"

The woven pieces Amanda created on the loom were exceptional not only because of her skill as a weaver, but also because she used yarn she had washed, carded, and spun herself of wool gathered from sheep raised on her family's ranch. Through her weavings, she expressed her identity as a Finnish American, bringing together the heritage of her homeland through Finnish techniques and her patriotism for her new adopted country. During World War I, the *Belt Valley Times* featured an article on Kraftenberg's work. "The yarn is heavier, softer, and warmer than any which can be purchased. . . . The socks are sure to outlast several pairs of socks knitted from manufactured yarn. Mrs. Kraftenberg is to be especially complimented upon the true American spirit which prompted her to go to all the labor which makes it possible for her to do her 'bit' for the boys at the front."

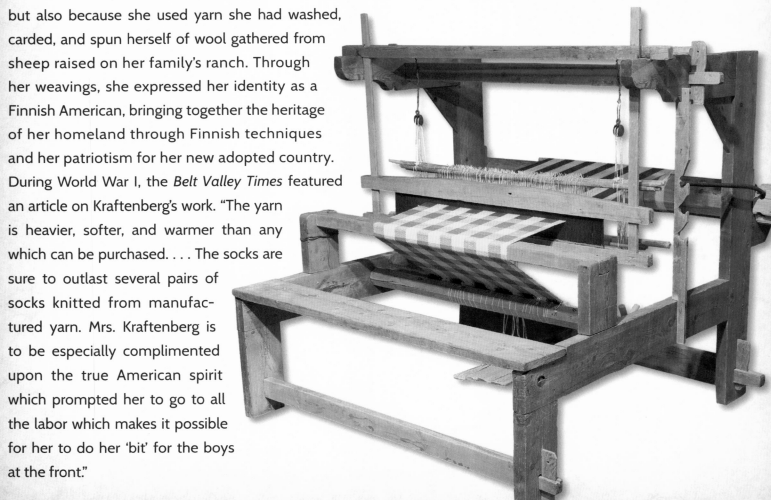

Weave on Your Own Homemade Loom

To weave, you must first make a loom. Cut a piece of cardboard about 7" x 9" and two 7" x ½" strips. At both 7" ends of your cardboard, measure evenly spaced lines with a ruler about ¼" apart 1" in from both ends, then cut slits on the lines. Glue the cardboard strips where the slits end on top and bottom.

Next you'll need to make the "warp." Start by threading yarn through the first slit on the left-hand side of one end. Tape the tail on the back side of the loom. Pull the yarn on to the matching slit on the other end, then wrap it around the back to the slit next to it. Repeat until you reach the last slit on the loom. Cut and tape the end piece on the back. You will now have vertical strings of yarn all across your loom.

Now you are ready to weave! Cut a piece of yarn about 1-2 feet long. Thread it through a needle and tie a knot at the end. You can weave with one string of yarn, or double it to make weaving go faster. Now start weaving horizontally with the needle, guiding the yarn first under and then over the warp strings of yarn. These horizontal rows are called the "weft." For the next row, start with over then under; alternate on each new row. Continue back and forth, pushing up the rows to keep them snug, until your yarn runs out or you want to start another color—but make sure you stop at the end of a row and leave the tail hanging. Start your new piece of yarn on the same side and leave a tail hanging. You can either tie the tails together or leave them to weave in at the end.

Continue weaving until you fill up your loom.

To take your weaving off the loom, first remove the tape off the tails on the back. Carefully pull your weaving to one end and remove it from the slits. Next, remove your weaving from the other end. Cut each loop and tie the ends together. This will make a fringe. If you want, you can add more fringe by threading a short piece of yarn on your needle, go through the edge of your weaving, cut, and tie ends together. Repeat until you get the amount of fringe you want.

WHAT YOU'LL NEED:

- Cardboard
- Ruler
- Pen or pencil
- Scissors
- White glue
- Yarn
- Large needle

Tipi Liner

Native drawings and paintings are also called pictographs. The pictures represent words, like an early form of writing.

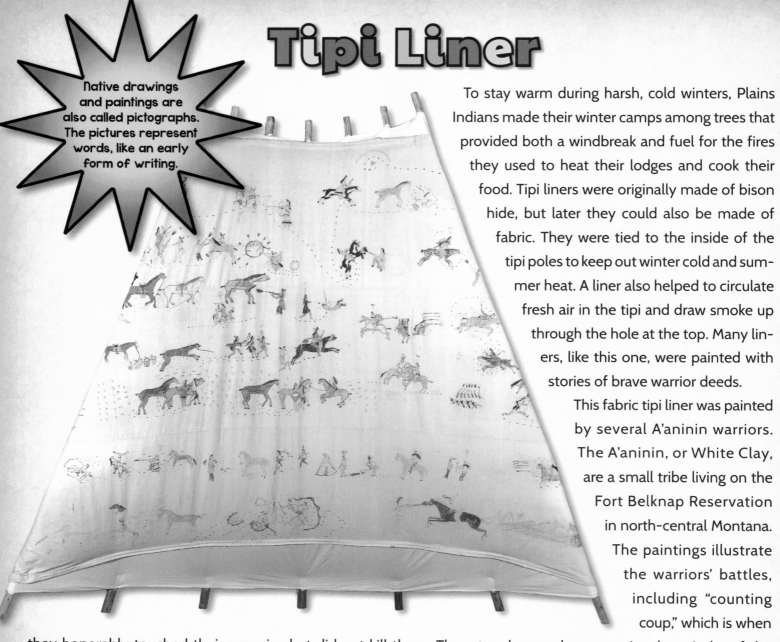

To stay warm during harsh, cold winters, Plains Indians made their winter camps among trees that provided both a windbreak and fuel for the fires they used to heat their lodges and cook their food. Tipi liners were originally made of bison hide, but later they could also be made of fabric. They were tied to the inside of the tipi poles to keep out winter cold and summer heat. A liner also helped to circulate fresh air in the tipi and draw smoke up through the hole at the top. Many liners, like this one, were painted with stories of brave warrior deeds.

This fabric tipi liner was painted by several A'aninin warriors. The A'aninin, or White Clay, are a small tribe living on the Fort Belknap Reservation in north-central Montana. The paintings illustrate the warriors' battles, including "counting coup," which is when they honorably touched their enemies but did not kill them. The artwork served as a continual reminder of the warriors' brave achievements.

In 1959, A'aninin elder Julia Ereaux Schultz gave this tipi liner to the Montana Historical Society. "I am proud of the Indian heritage in Montana," she said, "and I want future generations of Montana people to see some of the wonderful things left to us."

DRAW YOUR STORY SCENE

On the tipi liner below, draw your own story scene of when you did something brave or that you are proud of!

Weather Vane

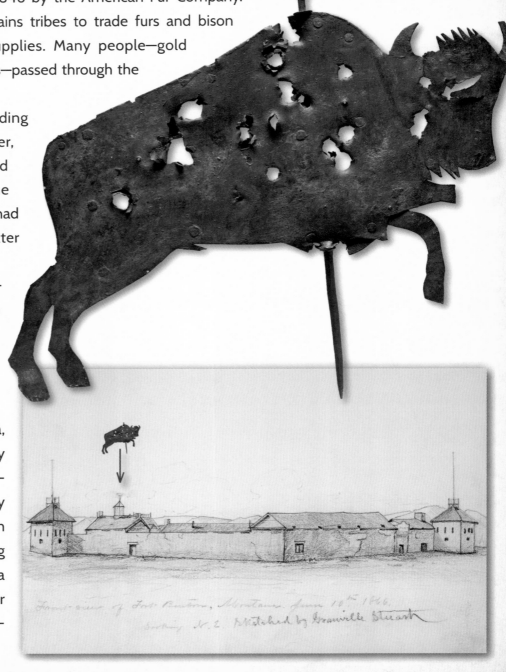

Old Fort Benton was founded in 1846 by the American Fur Company. It was a trading post for Northern Plains tribes to trade furs and bison hides for beads, guns, and other supplies. Many people—gold prospectors, road builders, and outlaws—passed through the fort on their way to other places.

The fort started as a small log building on the south bank of the Missouri River, but Major Alexander Culbertson agreed to the Blackfeet's request to move the fort to the north bank. Culbertson also had the fort built with adobe bricks for better protection against Montana's harsh weather. The finished fort had a two-story blockhouse on each end with portholes to shoot a cannon or rifles through for defense. It also had a trade store, warehouse, blacksmith and carpenter shops, a kitchen, and a barn. On top of the kitchen's cupola, shown here in an 1886 sketch by pioneer Granville Stuart, sat this sheet-iron bison weather vane, probably made by the fort's blacksmith. Although it's pretty beat up, missing one leg and used for target practice, it's a symbol of Montana's early frontier and a reminder of the state's first non-Indian settlement.

BUILD YOUR OWN WEATHER VANE!

First, draw a pattern of the two ends of an arrow, like the sample to the right. Trace them on colored construction paper and cut out.

Staple both arrow ends on a straw, then stick a pin through the center of the straw. Wiggle the pin so the straw spins around easily.

Next, fill a cup with dirt or sand. If you want, decorate your cup with a permanent marker. Stick a pencil with an eraser in the center of the dirt or sand. Firmly pack the dirt or sand. Then stick your arrow into the eraser with the pin.

Test your weather vane by blowing on it. If it tilts too much to one end, adjust your pin as needed to balance your arrow. Take it outside to see which way the wind blows!

WHAT YOU'LL NEED:

- Construction paper
- Scissors
- Plastic straw
- Pin
- Pencil with eraser
- Plastic cup
- Sand or dirt

Hat

As a soldier in Montana's 163rd Infantry Regiment during World War I, John L. Fogarty from Great Falls was sent to fight in France in December 1917. When he wasn't fighting, he liked to sing. Gaining confidence from the attention he received, he went to New York City after the war to pursue a singing career. He became known as the "Montana Minstrel." He was popular on the East Coast, and radio allowed his fans back home to enjoy his smooth voice. In 1932, his friends in Montana wanted to give him a special gift to remind him of home. They purchased this Stetson hat from a store in his hometown and had Great Falls artist O. C. Seltzer paint a scene with horses on the front and the Montana State Seal on the brim. Seventeen Montana livestock brands were added to the top, and 277 of his friends and fans signed it, including cowboys and judges, saloonkeepers and bankers, store workers and politicians, wool growers and the governor! Then the hat was sent to New York and presented to him on a special radio "Coast to Coast Broadcast over N.B.C." After Fogarty was given the hat, he made a short speech and then sang "In the Hills of Old Montana." The hat became his most prized possession, and he wore it to every performance, saying, "Every Theatre that I played, the hat got plenty of publicity."

In the 1950s, Fogarty retired after thirty years of show business. In 1966, he sent the autographed hat to the Montana Historical Society. He wanted it to remain in Montana long after he and his friends were gone. "This is the first hat of its kind," he said. "Rather than leave the hat with someone who don't appreciate my feelings about it, I thought that it would be in a place where it could be seen and appreciated for years to come." This special hat continues to show the heart of Montanans and their pride in the "Montana Minstrel."

MAKE AND DECORATE A PAPER HAT

First, cut a 6" hole in the center of a large paper plate. Put a paper bowl into the hole and glue the rim to the plate. The curved edge of the plate can hang down, like a bonnet, or curl up, like a cowboy hat. Staple it in a few spots to help hold it together while it dries. Once the glue is dry, paint your hat with poster paint or acrylic paint. You can paint it all one color or with designs in several colors.

Choose a piece of ribbon you like and glue it around the hat where the bowl and plate meet. Now decorate your hat with any craft supplies you have, like plastic flowers, feathers, foam shapes, sequins, rhinestones, glitter, etc. If you are making a Western hat like Fogarty's, draw a few made-up livestock brands with permanent markers.

If you and your friends make hats together, sign each other's hats. If you made it by yourself, write your friends' or family's names on it.

WHAT YOU'LL NEED:

- One 10" paper plate
- One 20-oz. paper bowl
- Scissors
- White glue
- Stapler
- Craft paint
- Ribbon
- Decorative craft supplies, like feathers, fake flowers, foam shapes, and glitter
- Permanent markers

Buffalo Jump

Due to changes in weather about 1,500 years ago, the number of bison (also called buffalo) on Montana's plains increased greatly. This was good fortune for Montana's Native people, who used every part of this important animal in almost every part of their life. From bison, they made food, clothing, tools, tipis, moccasins, blankets, saddles, bowstrings, thread, water bags, cups, soap, and hairbrushes. They even used dried bison poop as a fire starter. Because early people couldn't just go to the store, they used bows and arrows and natural landscape formations called pishkuns (buffalo jumps) to hunt the bison. The tribe's hunters at the top of the buffalo jump stampeded the bison over the cliff, and then men at the bottom killed any survivors. Working nearby, women prepared the meat, hides, and other parts for use.

There are buffalo jumps throughout Montana east of the Continental Divide, but Ulm Pishkun Buffalo Jump, located in First Peoples Buffalo Jump State Park near Great Falls, is probably the best known! It was used by tribal people in the area between AD 900 and 1500. This diorama illustrates how this site was used.

MAKE AND PHOTOGRAPH A DIORAMA

A diorama is a scene made with three-dimensional objects, often to show a historical scene. But it can really tell any kind of story. To make your own diorama, set up your toys in a scene that tells a story. You can even color a background on a large piece of paper or poster board. Photograph your scene, then print and attach it below with tape or a glue stick.

Beaded Gloves

The Cree culture is one of the largest Native groups in North America, but most live in Canada. In 1885, a group of Cree led by Little Bear settled in north-central Montana, where they were often hired as ranch hands to break wild horses, brand cattle, and guard horse herds on the open range. Taking great pride in their work, they wore beautifully beaded gauntlet gloves (long, protective gloves), bracers (arm guards), leggings and chaps (protective leg coverings).

This pair of fringed gloves is decorated with Cree syllables and symbols stitched with glass beads.

BEAD YOUR OWN KNIT GLOVES

To make your own one-of-a-kind gloves, buy an inexpensive pair of knit gloves and bead them with your own designs! Stitching beads on fabric is called "bead embroidery."

To start, cut a piece of cardboard to fit inside your gloves so you don't accidentally stitch the front and back of your gloves together. That would make them pretty hard to wear!

Thread your needle and knot both ends together. Make sure your needle with thread is small enough to go through your beads. As long as they aren't too small, you can use any kinds of beads that you want.

To tie a knot, go down through the fabric, then up and through your two threads and pull. Now you can start beading. Add one bead or more to your thread, then sew down through the fabric. Come up through the fabric and repeat until you have the design you want!

WHAT YOU'LL NEED:

- Pair of knit gloves
- Cardboard
- Scissors
- Thread
- Needle
- Beads

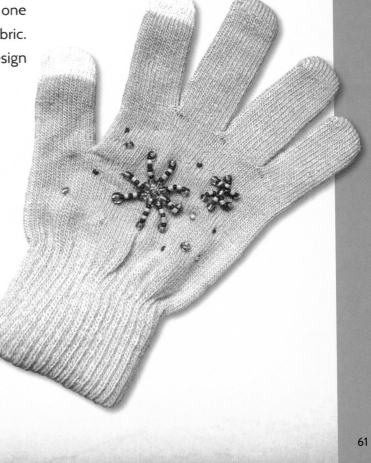

Quilt

Emma Louise Riley Smith was born in Arkansas in 1881, where her father was a farmer and former slave. Her grandfather always wanted them to "return to Africa"—which is what her family did when she was fourteen years old. They lived in Liberia, in West Africa, for fifteen years. Lonely after her parents and brother died, Emma and her younger sister returned to the United States to be with family members who had stayed.

After a brief time in Arkansas, they moved to Butte, where Emma married Martin Luther Smith in 1913. They then moved to Great Falls, where Martin worked as a cook for the Great Northern Railway and Emma was an active member of the African American Union Bethel Church. She served as president of the Women's Missionary Mite Society. A talented quilt artist, Emma often raffled her quilts off to raise money for the society.

One of her five children, Lucille Thompson, registered fourteen of Emma's quilts with the Montana Historic Quilt Project, which began in 1984 as part of a nationwide effort to preserve and record American quilting traditions. Emma had started this bright, colorful work, titled *Pineapple,* in Liberia and finished it in Montana.

Make a Paper Quilt

Make a decorative paper quilt! Start with a thick sheet of watercolor paper the size that you want your paper quilt to be. Think of the pattern you want to have. Squares are easy, and then you can cut them in half if you want. Or you can do another design, like the one with stripes below.

WHAT YOU'LL NEED:

- Thick watercolor paper
- Scrapbook or wrapping paper, or old magazine pages
- White glue or Mod Podge™
- Craft brush
- Permanent marker (optional)

If you are using squares for your quilt design, make a cardboard square pattern and then trace and cut squares out of scrapbook or wrapping paper, or colorful magazine pages. To plan your quilt design, draw a grid of squares on your watercolor paper. Then glue your squares (or cut-in-half triangles) with white glue or Mod Podge™ in a design that you like. If you want a shiny finish, apply a top coat of gloss Mod Podge™. Trim edges if needed and add solid lines or "stitch" marks with a permanent marker, if desired.

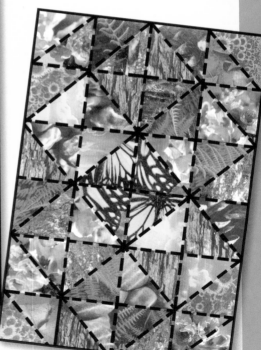

Chaps

Edward C. "Teddy Blue" Abbott was born in England, then moved to the United States with his parents in 1871. His father bought a herd of cattle in Texas and had them driven north to Nebraska, where the family had settled. Teddy Blue was just ten years old when he became a young "cowpuncher," which is another word for cowboy. He was a sickly child. Thinking it would make him stronger, his father had him ride with the cattle drivers on their long journey from Texas to Nebraska.

In 1883, Teddy Blue drove a herd of Texas longhorns to Montana. He felt at home in the breathtaking open landscapes and decided to stay. But in 1887, an extremely cold winter killed many herds of cattle. It reminded the cowboys that although beautiful, Montana country could also be brutally dangerous!

Teddy Blue told stories about the hardships, harsh weather, and many dangers involved with working cattle in his book, published in 1939, *We Pointed Them North: Recollections of a Cowpuncher.* But even though the life of a cowpuncher was hard, he also spoke of the bright side, saying, "Old-timers have told all about stampedes and swimming rivers and what a terrible time we had, but they never put in any of the fun, and fun was at least half of it."

In recalling the fun, he included songs and amusing stories of some of the people he met, like the famous painter Charles M. Russell, "Buffalo Bill" Cody, and Connie the Cowboy Queen, who was known to wear a funny dress with all the cattle brands of the region on it.

After cowpunching for years, Teddy Blue went to work for Granville Stuart—also known as "Mr. Montana"—who owned one of the largest ranches in the state. It's where he met and fell in love with Stuart's daughter, Mary. They got married and settled their own ranch called 3 Deuces Ranch near Lewistown. His chaps, shown here, are a reminder of Teddy Blue's cowboy spirit and a time when cowpunchers drove cattle on the open range.

WRITE A STORY ABOUT A FAVORITE EXPERIENCE

Travel Journal

On August 10, 1903, naturalist Hester Henshall and her husband Dr. James A. Henshall, superintendent of the U.S. Fisheries Station near Bozeman, boarded a train for Yellowstone National Park. The train brought them from Bozeman to Livingston, where they saw the new Northern Pacific Railway depot, and then on to Gardiner where travelers from around the world met with guides to take them into our first national park.

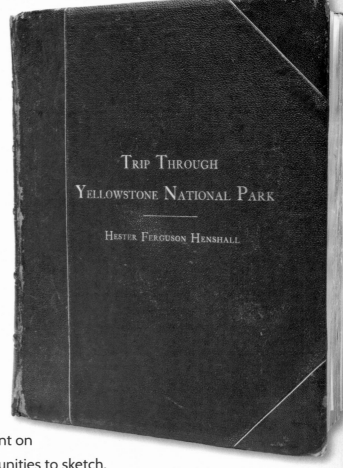

The Henshall's trip was organized by the Wylie Transportation Company. The couple boarded their stagecoach, which took them under the arch recently dedicated by President Theodore Roosevelt, and then on to their campsite. Hester recorded their trip in this journal. She described the camp as "a group of tents arranged to form a small village." The large tents had wooden floors and comfortable beds, hot water for baths, and a stove for warmth. There was a separate dining tent and evening entertainment around the campfire.

As they traveled from camp to camp, stagecoach drivers told stories to amuse their guests and stopped at merchants who offered goods and souvenirs along the way. The travelers also went on guided hikes with sweeping views of wildflower fields and opportunities to sketch.

Hester recorded many details of their trip in her journal, such as the route they took, which is still popular today, from Mammoth Hot Springs to the Hoodoos, Gibbon Meadows, Old Faithful, the Punch Bowl, Yellowstone Lake, Grand Canyon Falls (today's Upper and Lower Falls of the Yellowstone), and back to Gardiner. She wrote of experiences with their traveling companions and attempted to capture how the amazing views in the park affected her. Of Upper Falls, she wrote, "How can I describe the matchless wonder and beauty of it all[?] . . . I sat breathless; I could not speak. I did not want to talk, and did not want any one to speak to me; the tears ran unheeded down my cheeks. . . ."

Filled with personal accounts of their trip, nature sketches, and pictures cut out of guidebooks, Hester's Yellowstone journal provides a glimpse of the experiences of the park's early 20th-century tourists.

Make and fill a journal

There are many different kinds of journals. You can make a travel journal, like Hester's, to document experiences on a special trip. Or you can make a nature journal to draw sketches and record observations on visits to a local park or in your own yard. You can make an art journal to draw and paint in. You can make a writing journal for stories and poems. You can make an ideas journal to brainstorm in. And you can make a "happy" journal of pictures cut out of magazines, drawings, and notes of things, people, and places that make you happy.

To make your journal, collect sheets of 8.5" x 11" paper—they don't all need to be white. Try mixing in colored pieces of construction paper, tissue paper, and watercolor paper with plain, white paper. If they are too big, you can cut them down. Fold your stack of papers in half and punch holes near the folded edge. Make the cover a little larger so it covers your stack of folded pages. Decorate and punch holes in your cover to line up with the interior pages. If you decorate your front cover with three-dimensional features, like the tissue paper heart below, write or draw on your right-hand pages, where the surface is flat, and glue in objects like leaves, pictures, or mementos on the left-hand side, where you don't need a flat surface.

Bind your journal with string or brad fasteners, or you can staple it if your journal is not too thick. Enjoy!

WHAT YOU'LL NEED:

- Assorted papers
- Hole punch
- Craft supplies to decorate the cover
- String, brad fasteners, or staples to bind

Binoculars

These binoculars belonged to the famous mountain man, guide, and scout Jim Bridger. Jim was born in Richmond, Virginia, and moved to St. Louis, Missouri, with his family. At age eighteen, he left home to explore the West with the Rocky Mountain Fur Company expedition led by W. H. Ashley. He proved himself to be a natural at wilderness navigation and survival skills and was quick to understand American Indian languages and cultures. Over the next twenty years, Bridger traveled throughout the West as a trapper, guide, and scout. He is believed to be the first Euro-American to see the Great Salt Lake in Utah, and he told stories about the geysers and other wonders of what today is Yellowstone National Park.

Bridger often lived with local tribes and married a woman named Cora, the daughter of a Flathead Indian chief. In 1843, he and Louis Vasquez established Fort Bridger on the Oregon Trail in what is now southwest Wyoming. Cora died tragically, and Bridger later married the daughter of a Shoshoni chief. He then worked as a guide and a scout during the early Indian Wars.

Bridger is credited with being the first non-Native to see the Great Salt Lake

In 1863, because of his extensive knowledge of the region's wilderness, Bridger was asked to blaze a trail through the Bighorn Basin from the Oregon Trail to Montana Territory's gold fields at Virginia City. The better-known Bozeman Trail was often raided by Sioux, Cheyenne, and Arapaho warriors. Bridger himself guided two wagon trains along his route. After a life of adventure during the early days of the western frontier, Bridger died on his farm near Kansas City, Missouri, in 1881 at the age of seventy-seven.

Today, Montana's Bridger Mountain Range bears his name. These binoculars are a reminder of the legendary mountain man and his explorations of the West.

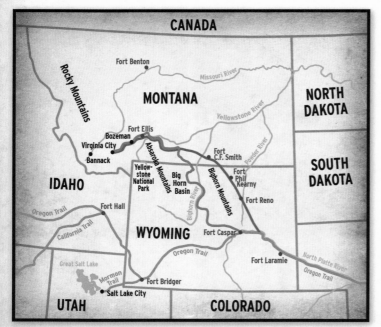

BRIDGER TRAIL
BOZEMAN TRAIL
OREGON/MORMON/CALIFORNIA TRAILS

MAKE CARDBOARD BINOCULARS

Pretend you are an explorer with these cardboard binoculars!

First, paint two cardboard tubes with poster paint, watercolors, or acrylic—whatever you have. Let dry.

Next, glue paper rolls together, then attach a paper clip on each end. With a craft brush, apply glue all over center part of tubes. Wrap tubes together with string, twine, yarn, or ribbon. Set aside until glue dries. Decorate your binoculars with any craft supplies you have on hand. Add decorative tape, lace, glitter, foam shapes, etc.

Cut a piece of string about 20" long. Punch one hole on the outside of each roll about 1/2" from the top, then tie each end of your string to each hole to make your neck strap.

Now you are ready to take your pretend binoculars on a nature walk at your local park or in your backyard. What can you spot through the two holes? Look for birds and other animals, insects, and flowers.

WHAT YOU'LL NEED:

- 2 cardboard rolls left over from toilet paper
- Craft paint
- White glue
- 2 paper clips
- String, twine, yarn, or ribbon
- Craft decorating supplies like decorative tape, ink pens, lace, foam shapes, etc.
- Hole punch

Doll

Like kids everywhere, Plains Indian children played with dolls. Early indigenous doll makers used natural materials around them to make their dolls. After European traders arrived, doll makers included trade goods, like beads, into their traditional patterns. By the middle of the 20th century, Native dolls became a popular souvenir for non-native people, which provided doll makers with needed income—especially important during the Great Depression.

This doll was made by an Assiniboine doll maker with supplies available in northeast Montana at the turn of the 20th century. She is thirty-six inches high, which is taller than most traditional dolls. Her head is carved from wood, then painted. Her hair is made of horse hair and braided. She wears clothing made of cotton and silk that Assiniboine women wore at the time, detailed with a traditional studded belt, knee-length red-and-white beaded necklace, and green moccasins decorated in Fort Belknap-style beadwork. The attention to detail continues on her back (which you can't see here) with a small buckskin purse, a diamond-shaped pouch, a knife sheath, and an awl case.

Although much about the doll's history is not known, she was probably traded for supplies to the grandparents of O. C. and Edith Worthy Johnson, who operated the first general store in Wolf Point, which served the nearby Fort Peck and Fort Belknap Reservations.

Native American dolls were not only for play. They were also a culturally significant form of art. Since they were dressed in the tradition of the doll maker's tribe, dolls became a record of Native American life.

MAKE A DOLL

To make your doll, paint a face, hair, and neck at one end of a paper towel roll. Apply glue around the inside top of the paper towel roll. Make a ball out of a piece of paper towel and stuff it inside to form the rounded top of your doll's head, then paint it with your doll's hair color.

To make your doll's yarn hair, wrap yarn around a piece of cardboard. Carefully remove the yarn loop and tie a piece of yarn around the middle. Cut the loops at each end and glue the hair on top of your doll's head.

Now you can make your doll's clothes and arms! Wrap and glue fabric around your doll's body, then decorate. Insert a pipe cleaner through the paper towel roll and clothes at its shoulders. Add craft-stick hands and feet, if you like.

WHAT YOU'LL NEED:

- Paper towel roll
- Craft paint
- Paintbrushes
- White glue
- Paper towel
- Yarn
- Felt or other fabric
- Other craft supplies for decorating, like beads, foam shapes, wood craft sticks, etc.
- Pipe cleaner

Teddy Bear

For centuries, children around the world have played with, cuddled, and slept with their favorite stuffed toys.

Stuffed animals were first sold commercially by the German company Steiff in the 1880s. Inspired by the story of President Theodore Roosevelt deciding not to kill a bear on a hunting trip, a couple from New York City made the first stuffed teddy bear in 1902. They named it "Teddy's Bear" after the president. As teddy bears became popular, more companies started making them.

In 1927, Rachelle Kelberer's parents gave her this teddy bear. She was just ten months old. The teddy bear was named "Taddy"—perhaps because that's how the young girl first pronounced Teddy.

Throughout the years, Taddy survived many trials, like when a teething Rachelle gnawed repeatedly on the bear's ear, and when the family dog chewed the bear so completely that the eyes, nose, mouth, and some of the clothing had to be replaced. Throughout it all, Taddy was Rachelle's cherished companion—there for her in tough times like when she was hospitalized for pneumonia at just five years old.

After Rachelle grew up, Taddy sat on her desk until he went to his new home at the Montana Historical Society. He's a reminder of the special bond between a child and a beloved toy.

Make a Teddy Bear

To make your own teddy bear, photocopy the white pattern to the right at 400% and cut out. Trace on two 9" x 12" pieces of felt and cut out for your front and back teddy bear pieces.

Cut out and glue on your bear's basic clothes, if you want your teddy to have them. Sew around the edges of your bear's body to hold the front and back together. Don't sew the edges of the head yet. A simple running stitch is easiest, poking your needle up through the fabric, then down through the fabric next to it, pulling your thread to make a stitch. Repeat. Once you've sewn all around the body, fill by pushing small bits of stuffing through the open head seam, starting with the arms and legs. A wooden spoon handle will help you get the stuffing into those small areas. Then fill the body.

Next, sew around the head. Leave an opening to add stuffing, starting with the ears, then the rest of the head. Sew the opening closed. Now you are ready to make your bear's face and decorate its clothing!

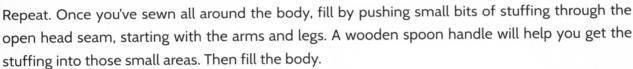

WHAT YOU'LL NEED:

- Photocopy of bear
- Two 9" x 12" pieces of felt
- Pen
- Scissors
- Assorted colors of felt
- White glue
- Embroidery floss or thread
- Sewing needle
- Polyester toy stuffing
- Craft supplies for decorating, such as googly eyes, lace, and ribbon

Hagen Site Artifacts

Rim of Cord Pottery

Chert Projectile Point

Chert Drill

Bone Awl

Bone Awl with Drill Hole

In 1937, an archaeologist named Oscar Lewis noticed bones, pieces of pottery, and stone flakes scattered on land near Glendive owned by Mayor Thomas Hagen. Lewis reported his findings to the Montana Archaeological Survey, and excavation began a year later.

The Hagen site was unusual in that it had evidence of permanent living structures, crop seeds, and agricultural tools made of bison bones. It was one of only two permanent village sites excavated in Montana. Most early people in what would become Montana did not live in permanent villages, but rather lived a nomadic life, taking their tipi homes with them whenever they moved.

Dating back to around 600 years ago, artifacts found at the Hagen site tell the story of the people who lived there. Most archaeologists believe the site belonged to early Crow who split from the Hidatsa (who now live in North Dakota) and became bison hunters. The cord-wrapped style of pottery found at the site, which is rare in the Missouri River Valley, is evidence that the people who made it were likely descendants of tribes from the Great Lakes region, who were pressured by other tribes to move west into Montana's bison country.

Today, the Hagen site is one of Montana's most important historic places. It was designated a National Historic Landmark in 1964.

Paint with Handmade Nature Tools

Make your own tools for creating art! Go on a nature walk in your backyard or local park. Collect sticks and different kinds of leaves and flowers.

Next, tie a plant to the end of each stick with a piece of string or twine, and you have made a nature paintbrush!

Pour craft paint into paper bowls, dip in your paintbrush, and paint away! Don't worry about painting anything realistic—just appreciate the shapes and colors your nature paintbrushes make.

You can enjoy your painting as is, fold it in half to make a card, or use it as fun, homemade wrapping paper for a special present.

WHAT YOU'LL NEED:

- Sticks
- Plant cuttings
- String or twine
- Craft paint
- Paper bowls
- Paper to paint on

Pocket Watch

The Northern Pacific Railway was the first transcontinental railroad across the northern United States. It ran from Lake Superior to the Pacific Ocean, through the rugged badlands in North Dakota, over the steep Continental Divide in the Rocky Mountains of Montana, and then over the Cascade Mountains in Washington. It transported farm products, home goods, cattle, and timber. Passenger service began in the 1880s. With its famous "Yellowstone Park Line," the NPR was the first railroad to bring passengers to a national park.

At the start of the 20th century, John Voorhies of Glendive worked as a railroad conductor for the Northern Pacific. He used this pocket watch with the railroad's red-and-black logo to time the trains, making sure they ran on schedule.

Because trains traveled very long distances—and were so much faster than horses—a consistent way of measuring time was needed. Before railroads were developed, most people used the sun's position in the sky to guess local time, or they'd refer to a clock tower or clock at the local watchmaker in town. Railroads used their own time measurements to coordinate their many trains traveling cross-country. By 1883, with so many different time zones—over 100 local and 53 railroad time zones—time coordination had become difficult for businesses and travelers.

In 1883, railroad companies created the Standard Time System, dividing the country into four time zones, one hour apart, from east to west. It required timekeepers to be exact, because when trains ran off schedule, they could run into each other, causing terrible accidents. By 1893, strict specifications and inspections were required for railroad pocket watches, like this one.

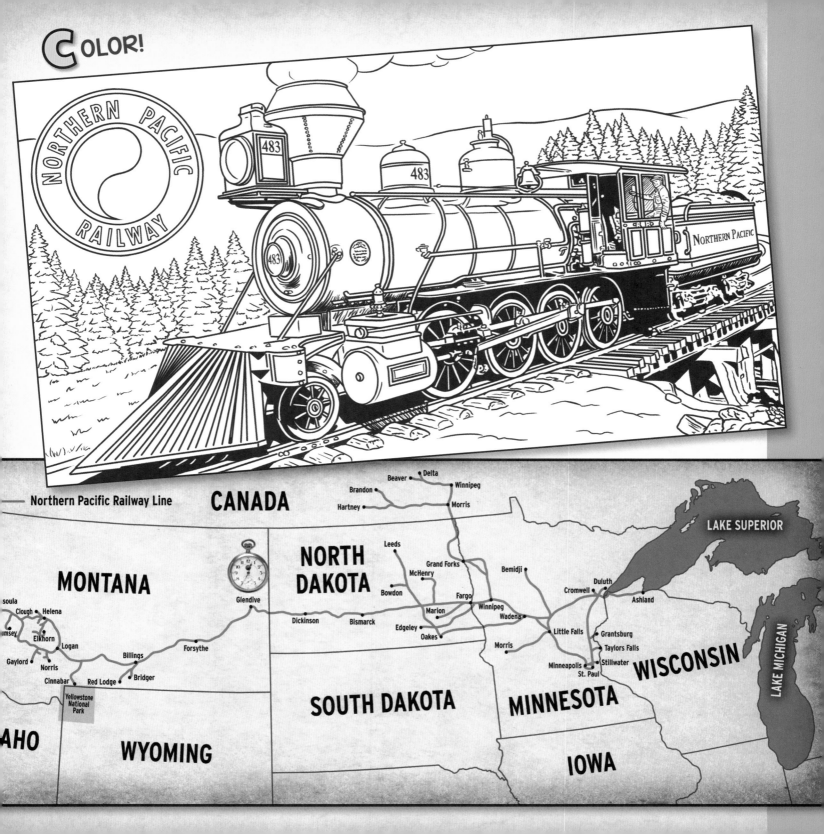

COLOR!

NORTHERN PACIFIC RAILWAY

483

NORTHERN PACIFIC

Northern Pacific Railway Line

CANADA

LAKE SUPERIOR

MONTANA

NORTH DAKOTA

Delta
Beaver
Brandon   Winnipeg
Hartney   Morris

Glendive

Leeds

Grand Forks
McHenry
Bowdon   Bemidji   Duluth
Cromwell   Ashland
Dickinson   Bismarck   Marion   Fargo
Edgeley   Winnipeg   Wadena
Oakes   Little Falls   Grantsburg
Morris   Taylors Falls
Minneapolis   Stillwater
St. Paul

soula
Clough Helena
umsey
Elkhorn Logan
Gaylord Norris   Billings   Forsythe
Cinnabar Red Lodge Bridger

Yellowstone
National
Park

AHO   WYOMING

SOUTH DAKOTA

MINNESOTA

WISCONSIN

LAKE MICHIGAN

IOWA

Buffalo Robe

For centuries, Plains Indian men painted story scenes about their heroic deeds, not only on their tipis, but also on their clothing, like this buffalo robe. The bottom half of this robe was painted by White Swan, a young Crow warrior who was one of six Crow scouts assigned to the 7th Cavalry of the U.S. Army in 1876.

White Swan—also known as "White Goose" or *Mee-nah-te-hash* in the Crow language—was twenty-five years old when he served under Lieutenant Colonel George Armstrong Custer during the Battle of the Little Bighorn fighting against the Sioux and Northern Cheyenne. White Swan was seriously injured in the battle, leaving him crippled and unable to hear and speak for the rest of his life. In spite of his disabilities, he continued to serve as a scout for five more years. When he could no longer scout, he created drawings and paintings of important events in his life—often from the famous battle, but also from other events, like his brave deeds in battle between tribes shown here.

The painting on the top half was painted by a different artist—possibly by another Crow warrior and scout named Curley, who may have been White Swan's cousin. Curley was photographed wearing the robe in 1883 by F. J. Haynes. But the top half could have also been painted by two artists, Curley and Bird Far Away. The latter painted a tipi liner with realistic, three-dimensional shading on horses, as seen here, which is rare in this kind of art. The two halves are separated by a band of colorful beaded designs on a different hide from the rest of the buffalo robe. It possibly was left over from another piece of clothing. The beadwork features an "hourglass with broken circle" motif typically beaded by Crow women.

Native artists' work, like White Swan's, continues to serve as a reminder of their brave deeds, talent as artists, and the era they lived in.

COLOR THE LITTLE BIGHORN SCENE

White Swan created many drawings and paintings of the Battle of Little Bighorn, like this one on muslin. After he could no longer make a living as a scout, he made money by selling drawings he made on accounting ledgers to people who visited the Crow Reservation. Although he didn't sign his artwork, pieces credited to him are done in the same style and share many of

the same scenes as artworks known to be his. A favorite, recurring scene of his shows him before the battle holding a telescope while his warhorse stood nearby. Can you spot him in this painting?

One of the best ways to study an artist's work is to paint or draw one of their pieces. Color White Swan's Battle of Little Bighorn painting below!

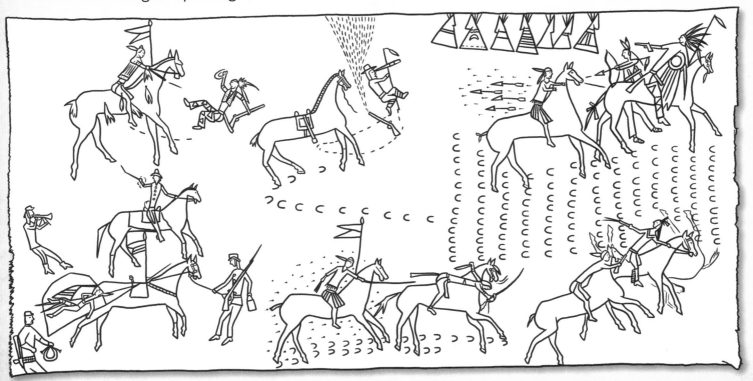

Camera

In 1891, Evelyn Cameron came to eastern Montana with her husband, Ewen, to raise polo ponies on a small ranch. But the ponies plan didn't work out, and their savings disappeared with the collapse of the Stock Growers National Bank in Miles City in 1893. They needed to find new ways to make money.

Ewen was an ornithologist who spent his time studying Montana's birds. Evelyn took care of the family's ranch, including cooking, gardening, selling produce, and taking in wealthy boarders. But her most successful business venture started when she bought her first camera in 1894. Over the next thirty years, Evelyn made some of Montana's most celebrated photographs. Often traveling for miles on horseback, she took pictures of people living on ranches and homesteads, cowboys driving cattle across the Yellowstone River, sheep being sheared, and farmers plowing the prairie. She charged twenty-five cents apiece for her prints.

Evelyn purchased this camera, a 5" x 7" Tourist Graflex, in 1905 and affectionately nicknamed it "Lexie." It had knobs to adjust the shutter speed as fast as 1/1000th of a second, which allowed her to take clear photographs of fast-moving subjects like bucking horses. In her diaries, she recorded notes of subjects, camera settings, lighting, and the type of negative she used.

Together, Evelyn Cameron's photographs and diaries provide a remarkable record of her life and of eastern Montana in the late 1800s and early 1900s.

Make a Pinhole Camera

The earliest pinhole cameras were not intended to take photographs but to study optics—the study of light and sight. Ancient pinhole cameras were literally room-sized! Cameras like these are called *camera obscura,* which is Latin for "dark room." You can learn how they work with a dark chamber from a round container, a tiny hole for light to travel through, and a screen to see the light's projection.

To make your pinhole camera, take the lid off your round container and set aside. Mark a 2" line around the bottom of the container. Have an adult help you cut along the line to separate the tube into two pieces. Punch a hole with a pushpin through the bottom of the small end. If your lid is whitish but still see-through, it will make a good screen. If it is completely clear, add wax paper to make it a semitransparent screen. Attach your lid to the open part of the small piece, then tape the long piece to that. Wrap foil all around the cut/lid area and tape with duct tape. Now, take your pinhole camera outside on a bright, sunny day. Close one eye and look through your tube with the other. You'll want to block as much light out of the tube as possible, so cup your hands around your eye and the camera. Look around and you'll see everything upside down on the screen inside your pinhole camera!

So how does the pinhole camera work? The pinhole acts as your camera's lens. It allows light rays to travel through a very small, single point. Light that normally travels in a straight line to your eyes intersects, or crosses, as it goes through the pinhole so the top becomes the bottom, making an upside-down projection on the screen inside your camera. Photographs can be made with pinhole cameras, but because the hole is so small, exposure to the film can take hours, or even weeks!

WHAT YOU'LL NEED:

- Round chip or breadcrumbs container with lid
- Pen or pencil
- X-Acto knife or utility knife
- Pushpin
- Wax paper (if lid is clear)
- Aluminum foil
- Duct tape

Look through → open end

Light travels ← through pinhole

Upside-down projection → on screen

Cowboy Poetry

Memories of the range
By D. J. O'Malley N bar N Kid

I long for the brakes of Sunday creek
For the flats on the Little ~~Dry~~ Dry
Thoughts of the Sage brush on Porcupine
Oft causes me to sigh
And I think of the days on the wide open range
Good days Now long gone by, but when
Happy and free as a human Could be
I rode for the N bar N

I oft think of Cowboys who rode with me there
On the roundup we rode each spring
A gay careless crew, brave hearted and true
Their friendship was as a steel ring
But where are they Now? They have Crossed the divide
All have dis-appeared from Mortal ken
Of that gay happy crew 'twould be hard to find two
Who rode for the N bar N

Cowboy poetry was first enjoyed as campfire entertainment for cattle drivers in the American West. It's known for its story-telling with humor, as well as sorrow.

The best cowboy poetry was written by actual cowboys who rode the range, like this one titled "Memories of the Range," by Dominick John "D. J." O'Malley, who was also known as The N Bar N Kid White.

O'Malley was born in New York City in 1867. After his father died in 1869, his mother, Margaret, married a soldier who was transferred in 1871 to Fort Keogh in Montana Territory. Soon after, he abandoned his new family and Margaret moved with her children to Miles City, where D. J. worked as a horse wrangler at the N Bar N Ranch. Between 1881 and 1896, O'Malley drove cattle from Texas to Montana and worked as a horse wrangler on the range and for neighboring ranches.

From the 1880s until 1943, O'Malley wrote many poems that told of the glory days of the open range. Most spoke of his time at the N Bar N Ranch and on cattle drives. His most famous poems include "A Cowboy's Death," "Cowboy's Soliloquy," and "After the Roundup." The last was made into a popular song called "When the Work Is All Done This Fall."

O'Malley's cowboy poetry lives on, offering a glimpse of life on Montana's open range in the late 19th century and preserving expressions still used in cowboy culture today.

RITE YOUR FAVORITE POEM

On the lines below, write your favorite poem. It can be your own original poem, one from a book, or even from a song—lots of songs are also poems! Think about what you like about the poem—the way it rhymes, it's rhythm, what it makes you think about, or how it makes you feel.

If you want to write your own poem, an online rhyming dictionary and thesaurus can help.

Game

Faro was the most popular gambling game in the Old West during the 19th century. Almost every saloon had a table for playing it. The game was often rowdy, with many excited players who were drinking beer and whiskey.

The game board had thirteen rectangles with a suit of card ranks from two through ten, and jack, queen, king, and ace painted on felt. Players placed their bets with chips on the thirteen rectangles, guessing whether that rank would win or lose. Two cards were dealt face up. Bets placed on the first card lost and those on the second won. An abacus-like counting system called a "casekeep" would keep score of the cards dealt. Notice that each row of beads is next to a rank that matches the cards on the board? When a card was dealt, the casekeeper would slide the bead corresponding to the rank of the card to the left if it won and to the right if it lost. It helped them to keep track of which cards were dealt, and therefore which cards were left to bet on. Since there are four suits (spades, clubs, diamonds, and hearts) of each card rank in a fifty-two-card deck, once all four suits in that rank were dealt, it was closed. Players would keep betting on the open ranks until the last three cards. Then they would guess which order they would be dealt in.

Faro is rarely played anymore, but this game set from the old Montana Saloon in Miles City is a reminder of those Wild West days.

TRY A NEW CARD GAME

Have you ever tried playing **Slap Jack**? You need a deck of cards and at least two players. Deal out all the cards face down to the players, one card at a time, so each has a stack of cards. Starting to the left of the dealer, the player lays down one card face up in the center of the table. Continue clockwise with each player laying a face-up card on the stack one at a time until someone lays down a jack—then everyone tries to SLAP THAT JACK as fast as they can! The person who slaps it first wins the stack of cards and adds them face down to the bottom of their card stack. When a player runs out of cards, they have one last chance to SLAP JACK! If they don't slap it first, they are out. The other players continue playing until the winning player has all the cards.

In **Crazy Eights**, the player who gets rid of their cards first wins. In this game, eights are wild! Deal each player five cards, one at a time, starting with the player to the left of the dealer. The rest of the deck is placed in the center of the table. The dealer takes the top card from the stack and puts it face up in the center of the table starting a new stack. If it's an eight, put it in the middle of the first stack and turn over another card. Starting with the player to the left of the dealer, each player must lay a card on the face-up card, BUT

it must be the same rank or suit—or it can be an eight. So if the card facing up is a queen of hearts, you can lay down a card with any queen or a card with any heart, or any eight. If you don't have a card to play, you must keep drawing cards from the face-down stack until you get a card you can play. If the stack runs out of cards to draw, you can pass. If you can play but would prefer to draw extra cards from the face-down stack, you can do so. If an eight is played, the player must then specify what suit they want the next person to play. The next player must lay down a card of that suit or an eight. Keep playing until one player has no cards left. That's the winner! If you want to play several rounds, you can keep score and then declare a winner when a player reaches an agreed-upon number, like 200. Count the number of points from the cards in each player's hand: 50 points for an eight, 10 points for a face card (jack, queen, or king), 1 point for an ace, and the same points for the number on the other cards. Add up the points from all the players with cards, and that's the number of points the winner of each round gets.

Petroglyph

Petroglyphs are carvings in rock that Native people made as a way of communicating, like an early form of writing. While rock art can be enigmatic (hard to figure out), it offers clues about how people lived here before Euro-American settlers arrived: what animals they hunted and what tools they used, how they armed themselves and dressed for war, how they celebrated, and more. Native rock art is found all over Montana and is considered sacred.

Originally part of Ellison's Rock near Colstrip, this petroglyph is thought to date back to 1500 to 1600. It features a central figure—a warrior with a large shield—and smaller figures to the right and left. Images like these, classified as Timber Creek-style, have been found throughout the Northern Plains, which includes eastern Montana. The artist may have been a Crow or Hidatsa man. What do you think it tells us? Well, we can see that they have very large shields and no guns or horses. That tells us that these warriors most likely fought on foot. Horses started showing up on the plains in the 1700s, so this carving and the artist who carved it are from before that time. After the 1700s, when warriors started riding horses, their shields were smaller because the big shields were too hard to manage while riding.

Why do you think people made rock art? Often it was to tell stories of their people to preserve their history for other generations. Warriors and hunters told of their accomplishments, which gave them a higher status in their tribe—especially if the war or hunt was very dangerous. Documenting their bravery at ceremonies and with petroglyphs would help them obtain valuable goods, a favorable marriage, or a leadership position.

WHAT'S A PICTOGRAPH?

Pictographs are rock art similar to petroglyphs, but instead of carving into the rock, the artist paints on it. As with petroglyphs, people used pictures and symbols to tell stories of their lives, beliefs, and brave deeds, and used paints to decorate rocks, hides, clothing, pottery, tipi covers and liners, and more.

Make Your Own Petroglyph

It's fun and easy to make your own petroglyphs! First, you make a salt dough that will be your "rock." In a large bowl, mix flour, salt, and water. Knead it with your hands for five minutes until it forms a soft, easy-to-handle dough. If it is sticky, add a little more flour. If it is too dry to form a ball, add a little water. Let your dough rest for ten minutes, then split the dough into two or three pieces. The size of each piece will determine the size of your "rocks." Roll your dough in a ball and then press it lightly on a sheet of parchment paper to make a smooth surface.

WHAT YOU'LL NEED:

- 2¼ cups flour
- 1 cup salt
- 1 cup water
- Toothpicks
- Parchment paper
- Cookie sheet

Now you're ready to make your rock art—but what should you draw? It can be anything you like, maybe a picture of your family and pets, you and your friends playing a favorite sport, or a scene from a trip with your family. (Do not try carving on real rocks. You may hurt yourself!)

Use a toothpick to draw your picture into the dough. If you don't like it, that's okay. You can easily redraw it. Just roll your dough into a ball again, press to smooth, and try again. When you get a petroglyph you like, carefully transfer the parchment paper with your petroglyph to a cookie sheet for baking. Bake in the oven at 180 degrees for two hours, then let cool.

Comic Strip

Stan Lynde began drawing comics as a young boy growing up on his family's sheep ranch near Lodge Grass. As a young man serving during the Korean War, he drew comic strips for U.S. Navy publications. After the Navy, he continued to make comic strips. His most famous was called *Rick O'Shay*. It celebrated the Old West while also poking a little fun at it. The comic strip was distributed across the nation for twenty-three years—around 15 million people read it daily when it was at its peak of popularity. During his lifetime, Stan created many oil paintings, a memoir, an illustrated eight-volume Western mystery series, and more than 19,000 comic strips! The above comic was from a small box of original *Rick O'Shay* comic strips that survived a devastating fire in his Billings home. It offers a glimpse of the work of a prolific artist who was inspired by his Montana roots.

DRAW YOUR OWN COMIC STRIP!

Rolmonica

Before the 19th century, musical instruments generally needed a live performer. But by the turn of the century, music boxes evolved from musical clocks. They were the first musical instruments that didn't require a musician, but they had to be made by hand and were too expensive for most people. But with the Industrial Revolution, new manufacturing techniques allowed not only mass production of music boxes, which made them more affordable, but also other new musical instruments, like coin-operated machines for use at arcades and carnivals and smaller musical contraptions for personal use in homes, like this Rolmonica.

In 1928, the Rolmonica Music Company of Baltimore, Maryland, started manufacturing this "automatic harmonica" that played a music roll. It was advertised as "small in size . . . yet mighty in its finger-tickling, toe-tingling tune power." Anyone could play it, "for all you have to do is insert a roll, and turn the handle while you blow."

The Rolmonica was a modified harmonica made with a plastic mouthpiece to blow through and compartments to hold a roll of paper music. The music roll had holes in the paper that sounded different notes as air passed through them. Two handles on the side moved the music roll, so the notes made a song when you blew into it. The player could breathe in and out, and the Rolmonica played continuously.

In the 1932 Montgomery Ward & Co. catalog, Rolmonicas sold for one dollar and came with four rolls of music. Additional rolls came in sets of five, each costing forty-seven cents.

This Rolmonica has nine rolls of songs, including "Hot Time in the Old Town." It belonged to Kristine and Rhoda Hoverson, who grew up in what used to be the town of Ollie. Rhoda wrote, "I marvel that my parents, as little money as they had in those days [early 1930s], managed to provide us with such wonderful toys. . . ."

Make Homemade Musical Instruments

To make a kazoo, all you really need is a toilet paper roll, wax paper to cover the end, and a rubber band to secure the wax paper to the cardboard roll. If you want to decorate it, cut a piece of paper the length of your cardboard roll and wide enough to wrap around it. Color the paper and attach it to the roll with tape. Sing or talk through the open end to hear your kazooey sound!

To make a tambourine, paint a paper plate with a fun design. When dry, punch sixteen holes evenly spaced along the rim of the plate. Tie a bell on every other hole, and tie ribbon on the holes without bells. Now you are ready to play it: shake your tambourine to jingle its bells, and strike it with your hand or hip.

To make your guitar, cut a round hole in a cereal box and tape ends closed. Cut a paper towel roll to 6". To make the bridges, cut two pieces of cardboard 3½" x 1" and roll up. Paint all pieces. Once dry, cut ten notches in one end of your paper towel roll, five on front and five on back. Glue the paper towel roll to the top of the box. Add a bridge above and below the cut-out circle of your box. Let dry, then carefully string your rubber bands over the bottom of the box to the top of the paper towel neck, securing each rubber band in two (front and back) notches. Now you are ready to strum or pick your guitar strings. How many sounds does your guitar make? Rubber bands of different width and length will make different sounds.

Fishing Fly

Blessed with some of the best trout rivers in the world, Montana is fly-fishing country. Fish were a staple food of Montana's early people. Newcomers also noticed the abundance of fish. On the way to the Pacific Ocean, Captain Meriwether Lewis noted the area's abundance of trout when Private Silas Goodrich caught a half dozen of the fish near the Great Falls of the Missouri.

Another early visitor, British author Rudyard Kipling, came to Montana in 1889 and boasted that he gave up counting the trout he caught from the Yellowstone River after forty. He said they weren't big, but they fought like tigers!

Today fly fishing is not just a popular sport. It is very important to Montana's economy, bringing in about $400 million a year! State conservation regulations protect trout populations and their habitat so the sport can be preserved for future generations.

The technique of fly fishing is considered an art by many, as is making hand-tied flies. Fly-fishing enthusiasts often spend the long, cold winter months tying flies while dreaming of beautiful warm days fly fishing Montana's world-class streams and rivers like the Yellowstone, Missouri, Madison, Gallatin, Bighorn, Smith, and Blackfoot. Flies are often made to resemble insects the fish like to eat, like mayflies, caddisflies, or grasshoppers, but some people tie flies with crazy colors and patterns in hopes of exciting the fish.

This hand-tied, soft-hackle-pattern fishing fly made from hair and feathers was used by Nellie Walker Penhale and her family in the late 1940s to early 1950s. Fly-fishing objects in the Montana Historical Society collection celebrate the role of fishing in shaping Montana's identity in the past and into the future.

MAKE A FISHING GAME

Catch felt fish with a magnetic fishing fly! First, make your fish. Either draw your own fish patterns or make a photocopy of the fish patterns and fin to the right at 200%, then cut out. Trace your patterns onto different colors of felt, then cut out your fish and fins. Draw scales and fin details with a permanent marker. Glue on one googly eye and magnet per fish, then glue its fin on top of the magnet. Keep in mind magnetic polarity—which sides of the magnets pull together and which sides push away from each other. Test them first to make sure the top of the magnet glued on your fish attracts the magnet that will be on your fishing fly.

To make your fly, use pipe cleaners, feathers, embroidery floss, and other craft supplies. Glue a magnet to your fly so it attracts the magnet on the fish.

To make your fishing pole, find a stick and tie a string on it long enough to touch the floor when you are standing. Tie your fly to the end of the string.

Now you're ready to go fly fishing!

WHAT YOU'LL NEED:

- Fish pattern
- Felt
- Permanent marker
- Scissors
- Googly eyes
- Magnets
- Glue
- Craft supplies like pipe cleaners, feathers, and embroidery floss
- Long stick
- String

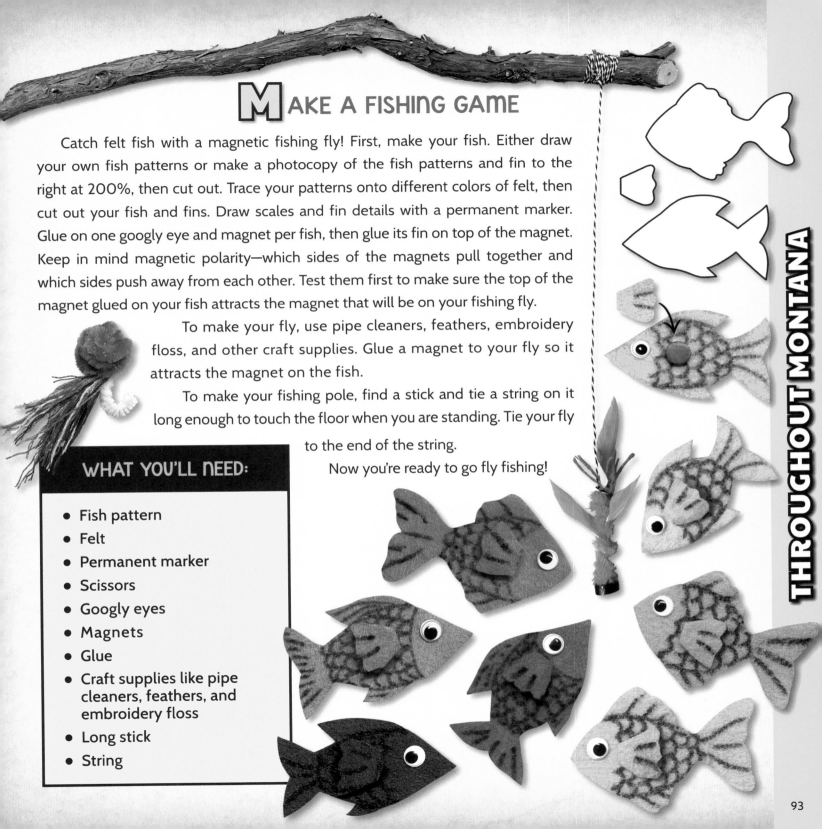

Cradleboards

Montana's tribal women used cradleboards to carry their babies on their backs, like a backpack, so the mothers could keep their arms free for other activities while making sure their baby was safe and cozy. The stiff wood back allowed the mother to prop up the baby and secure the cradleboard to tipi poles when she wasn't wearing it.

Designs and materials varied from tribe to tribe. The tan cradleboard, thought to be either Shoshone or Salish, is from about 1900. It features soft, pale buckskin attached to a wooden plank with brass tacks, flower designs made of glass seed beads, decorative fringe, laces to hold the baby in, and straps on the back.

The red cradleboard is from the Flathead Reservation and dates back to the late 1800s. It's said that it was used for a chief's baby! The high back is fully beaded in a floral design. It also has laces to hold the baby in, but they are covered by an extra red wool cloth that helped keep the baby warmer. And it has a soft hood to protect the baby's head.

What would your tribe's design look like?

MAKE A MINIATURE PAPER CRADLEBOARD—WITH BABY!

Start by making a copy of this page on 11" x 17" paper, preferably cardstock. Color your baby and cradleboard pieces, decorating them with your own designs. Cut out pieces and punch holes as shown. Staple right and left cradleboard cover pieces close to the edge of cradleboard back. String three pieces of yarn through each hole and tie to make a fringe. Wrap your baby in its (tissue paper) blanket and put inside its cradleboard, then cover baby with sides.

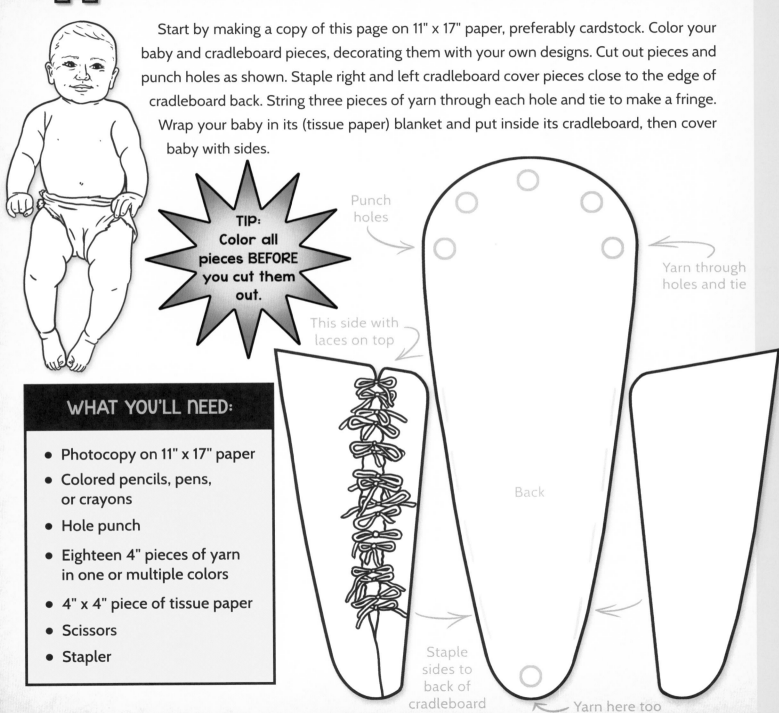

TIP:
Color all pieces BEFORE you cut them out.

Punch holes

Yarn through holes and tie

This side with laces on top

Back

WHAT YOU'LL NEED:

- Photocopy on 11" x 17" paper
- Colored pencils, pens, or crayons
- Hole punch
- Eighteen 4" pieces of yarn in one or multiple colors
- 4" x 4" piece of tissue paper
- Scissors
- Stapler

Staple sides to back of cradleboard

Yarn here too

Silver Service

After the Spanish-American War, the United States realized it needed a stronger navy with a new fleet of warships. Congress approved money for twelve ships, with one being the armored U.S.S *Montana*. Patriotism was strong, and in 1907, the Treasure State's legislature authorized $6,000 to have a grand silver service made to "enable the officers of the vessel to entertain official guests in a manner befitting the dignity of the State [of Montana]."

Dillon's Huber Brothers jewelers were hired to make the ornate silver service. They ordered nineteen hand-wrought silver pieces from Reed and Barton in Massachusetts. Then the jewelers decorated the pieces with not only nautical themes but also symbols of Montana, including bitterroot (the state flower), bison, and artwork by Charlie Russell.

The finished silver service was presented at the Norfolk Navy Yard in Virginia on November 11, 1908. In the following years, it was used for important events and guests, including President William Howard Taft, who sailed on the U.S.S. *Montana* for a visit to Panama in 1910. The silver service remained on board until the ship was decommissioned in 1921 and was then moved to the U.S.S. *Helena* until that ship was retired in 1963.

In 1987 the Navy gifted the silver service to the Montana Historical Society, where it serves as an elegant symbol of state and national pride.

Make an Ornate "Silver" Vase with Paper Flowers

To make your "silver" vase, start with a plain glass vase or jar. With the help of a parent, draw a decorative design on one side of the glass with glue from a low-heat glue gun. (Never use a hot glue gun. It can shatter the glass!) Let dry, then brush white glue all over the glass in a thin layer. Apply aluminum foil shiny-side up. With your hands, mold the tin foil around your raised design.

To make each flower, you'll need five pieces of tissue paper cut to 8" x 8". You can use colored tissue paper or white tissue paper stained in coffee, different colors of tea, or food coloring to make your own unique paper. To do this, crunch the pieces of tissue paper to form balls and quickly dip each into the liquid, then set on wax paper to dry. When your tissue balls have dried, carefully open and flatten.

With five sheets of paper together, fold them back and forth accordion style, then secure the folded end together with a pipe cleaner "stem." Trim the open end with a zigzag cut.

Finally, separate the sheets of paper to open your flower. Make more and fill your silver vase!

What You'll Need:

- Plain glass vase or jar
- Low-heat glue gun with glue sticks
- White glue
- Paintbrush
- Aluminium foil
- Tissue paper
- Coffee, tea, or food coloring (optional)
- Pipe cleaners
- Scissors

Mail Banner

When Montana was made a state in 1889, it already had over 600 post offices! Even so, people living in rural areas could not get adequate mail service. To have the right to have mail delivered directly to their country homes, Montanans joined the fight for Rural Free Delivery, and in 1896, Congress approved $40,000 for rural mail service across the nation. Farmers outside Billings were the first to successfully petition for free mail delivery to their homes. Other Montana rural communities followed. By the late 1930s, almost 180 rural mail carriers covered about 6,000 miles to deliver mail!

Rural mail delivery had other benefits too. Good roads were built for the postal routes, and mail carriers were known as the "eyes and the ears of rural communities." Since they visited people in remote locations regularly, they were known to watch out for people like the isolated elderly, and they made sure medicine and other important goods were delivered.

In spite of how important rural mail carriers were to remote communities, they received little money for the job. They were not paid for the upkeep of the horses or automobiles they needed to deliver the mail, and they covered many miles and worked long hours. In the winter a mail route could take two days, and the carrier would have to sleep at people's houses along the way!

Two groups fought for better pay and working conditions for rural mail carriers: the Montana Rural Letter Carriers Association (MRLCA) and the National Rural Letter Carriers Association (NRLCA). They had limited success until 1962, when they were formally granted the right to bargin as a group. The NRLCA was selected to represent them, making it one of the first public-sector trade unions.

This banner was displayed at the annual convention of the Montana Rural Letter Carriers Association. It's made of black silk, trimmed in gold braid and fringe. It features the Montana state flower—the bitterroot—and has a beautiful painted scene of mountains with a rural homestead. The banner represents not only the Montanans that fought for free rural mail delivery, but also the hardworking mail carriers—all who brought our rural communities together through the mail.

Make a banner

Make a banner declaring your favorite hobby or a job you want to do when you grow up!

Start by cutting a rectangle out of felt. You can make it any size you want. Cut a 1" piece of cardboard the width of your banner. Glue it on the back top of your banner. When the glue is dry, make a hole on each end through the cardboard and felt and tie a single piece of yarn, braid, or ribbon to hang it.

Now you are ready to decorate the front of your banner! You can make letters, symbols, and objects out of felt paint, fabric markers, and glitter. Get creative and have fun!

WHAT YOU'LL NEED:

- Felt
- Scissors
- Cardboard
- White glue
- String, yarn, or ribbon
- Craft supplies for decorating, like fringe, paint, fabric markers, glitter, etc.

Modern *Woman*

Woman, by Willem de Kooning, was the first of many modern art pieces given to the Montana Historical Society by George and Elinor Poindexter.

George was a third-generation Montanan who grew up in Dillon. He moved to New York City and became a successful businessman, and he and his wife owned and operated the Poindexter Gallery. Their gallery featured artwork of the "New York School"—a modern art movement mostly known for abstract expressionism by painters based in the city during the mid-20th century.

In 1960, George and Elinor decided to donate their art collection of ninety-eight paintings and one photograph to the Montana Historical Society. George said, "I hope that the pleasure they [these paintings] have given me will be shared by the people of my native state. . . . I have been collecting these pictures for ten years and I love them all. My reason for giving them away is because my whole family were always Montanans at heart and I'd like to do something for the state. I believe the collection is good enough and varied enough to have an effect on Montana's cultural climate."

Willem de Kooning was one of the most important artists of the 20th century. Other modern masterpieces from the Poindexters' collection include pieces by artists such as Jackson Pollock, Franz Kline, Richard Diebenkorn, Sonia Gechtoff, and Robert DeNiro—father of the famous actor by the same name.

Since 1960, the Poindexters' gift of modern art has been shown in sixty-one exhibitions in fourteen states, from New York to California. It has provided ongoing inspiration and art history to Montanans, researchers, and artists across the country.

Make a modern art suncatcher

To make your modern art suncatcher, first cut up different colors of tissue paper into small geometric shapes.

Next, shape craft wire into a frame. Twist the ends together at the top with a loop or hook to hang your suncatcher. When you are satisfied with your shape, cut two pieces of clear, adhesive shelf paper a little larger than your wire shape. Lay one piece on your work surface, sticky side up, then lay your wire frame over it.

Now add the geometric pieces of tissue paper to the shelf paper. Make sure you put tissue paper only inside the wire frame, and try to lay the tissue paper down in a single layer with little or no overlap. This will make it easier for the sun to shine through.

When you have filled your wire shape, carefully put your second piece of shelf paper over your wire frame, sticky side down, to sandwich the wire and pieces of tissue paper in between. Cut off excess shelf paper outside the wire frame, leaving a little border to seal around the wire. Tie a string to the top to hang your suncatcher in a window.

Clear adhesive shelf paper

Sticky side up

WHAT YOU'LL NEED:

- Colored tissue paper
- Scissors
- Craft wire
- Wire cutters
- Clear adhesive shelf paper
- String

Friendship Doll

In 1924, the U.S. Congress passed a law banning most people from Asia, including Japan, from entering the country. In turn, Japan grew less friendly toward America. The Reverend Sidney Gulick came up with the idea of promoting friendship and understanding through the two countries' children. In 1927, more than 12,000 American "blue-eyed dolls" were shipped to Japan to be given to elementary and kindergarten children. In return, Japan sent fifty-eight Japanese friendship dolls to be given to the children of America. This doll, called Miss Ishikawa, is one. She and her companions, dolls known as *tôrei-ningyô* in Japanese, made their voyage to San Francisco like little people, with passports and first-class tickets. Each had her own trunk packed with miniature furniture and personal items to make her comfortable in her new home in America.

The goodwill generated by the friendship doll exchange was short-lived. With the start of World War II, the Japanese government destroyed most of the American dolls. Few of the blue-eyed dolls and only forty-six of the Japanese dolls remain.

Today, dolls like Miss Ishikawa are a symbol of friendship and peace among nations.

MAKE A FRIENDSHIP BRACELET

First, cut five 12" strands of embroidery floss or thin yarn in different colors. Fold all in half and tie a loop at the folded end, as on the right. Tape the loop end on a table to hold the strands while braiding. Now you should have ten strands with two of each color. Keep each color of strands together while braiding. Starting with the left strands (1), go over the strands to the right (2), then under the strands in the middle (3). Your first strands will now be in the middle. Then do the same thing with the strands on the far right (5)—go over the strands to the left (4), then under the new strands in the middle. If you want to add pony beads, add them to the center three colors, then continue braiding.

Repeat braiding until your bracelet is long enough to go around your friend's wrist, then tie all strands together. To wear, wrap the friendship bracelet around your wrist and put the tied end through the loop end, then tie end.

Make a few bracelets to trade with your friends!

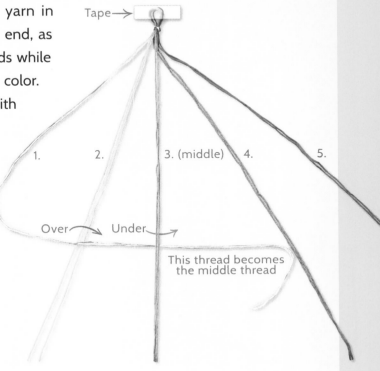

Tape →

1. 2. 3. (middle) 4. 5.

Over   Under

This thread becomes the middle thread

WHAT YOU'LL NEED:

- Embroidery floss or thin yarn in five colors
- Scissors
- Tape
- Plastic pony beads (optional)

Over 100 Places to Learn More About Montana History!

There are so many fun places to visit in Montana to learn about its history, from dinosaurs to Native Americans to gold-mining settlers. Some historic locations may be in your own town!

On the following pages, you can journal about favorite historical objects that you've seen in person. There's room to draw a picture of the object and write notes about what you learned or observed. Where and when did you see it? Who used it? When and how did they use it? Now you know how historical objects help us learn about our history!

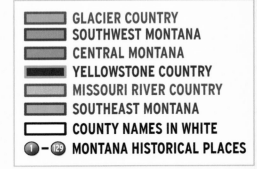

GLACIER COUNTRY
SOUTHWEST MONTANA
CENTRAL MONTANA
YELLOWSTONE COUNTRY
MISSOURI RIVER COUNTRY
SOUTHEAST MONTANA
COUNTY NAMES IN WHITE
1 – 129 MONTANA HISTORICAL PLACES

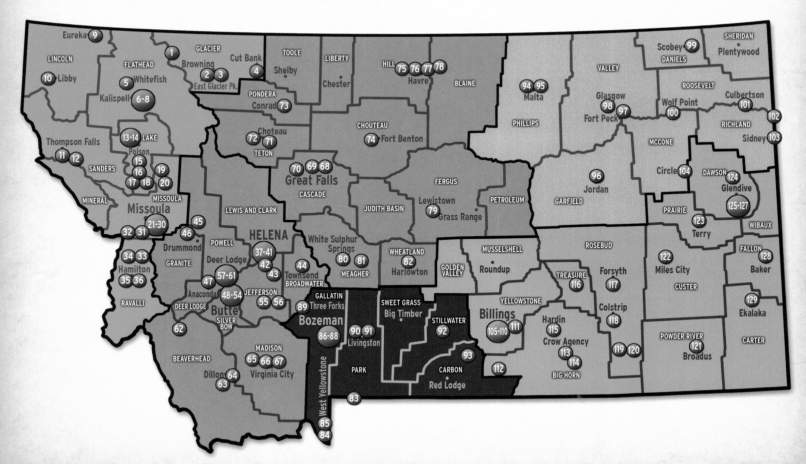

GLACIER COUNTRY

1. Glacier National Park
2. Museum of the Plains Indian, Browning
3. Diamond R. Brown Cowboy Museum, Browning
4. Glacier County Historical Museum, Cut Bank
5. Whitefish Depot
6. Conrad Mansion Museum, Kalispell
7. Northwest Montana History Museum, Kalispell
8. Hockaday Museum of Art, Kalispell
9. Tobacco Valley Historical Village, Eureka
10. The Heritage Museum, Libby
11. Sanders County Historical Society
     & Old Jail Museum, Thompson Falls
12. The Paradise Center, Paradise
13. Miracle of America Museum, Polson
14. Polson Flathead Lake Museum, Polson
15. Ninepipes Museum of Early Montana, Charlo
16. The People's Center, Pablo
17. National Bison Range Visitor Center, Moiese
18. St. Ignatius Mission
19. Swan Valley Museum, Condon
20. Seeley Lake Historical Museum and Visitor Center
21. Rocky Mountain Museum of Military History, Missoula
22. Historical Museum at Fort Missoula
23. Montana Museum of Art and Culture, Missoula
24. Montana Natural History Center, Missoula
25. Missoula Art Museum
26. Museum of Mountain Flying, Missoula
27. Smokejumper Visitor Center, Missoula
28. National Museum of Forest Service History
     Visitor's Center, Missoula
29. Montana Museum of Work History, Missoula
30. Rocky Mountain Elk Foundation, Missoula
31. Travelers' Rest Connection/State Park, Lolo
32. Holt Heritage Museum, Lolo
33. Stevensville Historical Museum
34. Historic St. Mary's Mission & Museum, Stevensville
35. Daly Mansion, Hamilton
36. Ravalli County Museum & Historical Society, Hamilton

SOUTHWEST MONTANA

37. Montana Historical Society, Helena
38. Montana State Capitol, Helena
39. Cathedral of St. Helena
40. Original Governor's Mansion, Helena
41. Holter Museum of Art, Helena
42. Jefferson County Museum, Clancy
43. Elkhorn State Park
44. Broadwater County Museum and Library, Townsend
45. Brand Bar Museum, Ovando
46. Garnet Ghost Town, near Drummond
47. Copper Village Museum & Arts Center, Anaconda
48. Butte Historic District
49. The World Museum of Mining, Butte
50. Copper King Mansion, Butte
51. Mineral Museum, Butte
52. Mai Wah Society, Butte
53. Piccadilly Museum of Transportation, Butte
54. Butte-Silver Bow Public Archives, Butte
55. Jefferson Valley Museum, Whitehall
56. Lewis and Clark Caverns State Park, near Whitehall
57. Grant-Kohrs Ranch National Historic Site, Deer Lodge
58. Powell County Museum, Deer Lodge
59. Old Prison Museum, Deer Lodge
60. Montana Auto Museum, Deer Lodge
61. Frontier Montana Museum, Deer Lodge
62. Big Hole National Battlefield, Wisdom
63. Bannack State Park, Dillon
64. Beaverhead County Museum, Dillon
65. Nevada City Historic District
66. Virginia City Historic District
67. Thompson-Hickman Museum, Virginia City

CENTRAL MONTANA

68. C.M. Russell Museum Complex, Great Falls
69. Lewis and Clark Interpretive Center, Great Falls
70. First Peoples Buffalo Jump State Park, Ulm
71. Old Trail Museum, Choteau
72. Two Medicine Dinosaur Center, Bynum
73. Conrad Transportation and Historical Museum
74. Fort Benton National Historic Landmark District
75. Rudyard Depot Museum
76. H. Earl Clack Memorial Museum, Havre
77. Havre Beneath the Streets
78. Blaine County Museum, Chinook
79. Central Montana Museum, Lewistown
80. Castle Museum and Carriage House,
     White Sulphur Springs

THE MONTANA DINOSAUR TRAIL

This dinosaur icon marks the fourteeen locations that make up the Montana Dinosaur Trail. Travel back in time through informative programs, field digs, and exhibits with interpretive displays, replica and real dinosaur skeletons, and other fossils that teach the story of the prehistoric creatures that once lived in the Treasure State. You can even get your own Montana Dinosaur Trail Prehistoric Passport from any location along the trail or online at https://mtdinotrail.org/prehistoric-passport. It's filled with information about the Montana Dinosaur Trail locations, cool Fun Fossil Facts, a field notes section, and a space to collect your official "Dino Icon" stamps.

81. The Charles M. Bair Family Museum, Martinsdale
 82. Upper Musselshell Museum, Harlowton

YELLOWSTONE COUNTRY

83. Yellowstone National Park
84. Grizzly and Wolf Discovery Center, West Yellowstone
85. Museum of the Yellowstone, West Yellowstone
86. Museum of the Rockies, Bozeman
87. American Computer and Robotics Museum, Bozeman
88. Gallatin History Museum, Bozeman
89. Missouri Headwaters State Park, Three Forks
90. Yellowstone Gateway Museum, Livingston
91. Livingston Depot Center
92. Museum of the Beartooths, Columbus
93. Clarks Fork Valley Museum, Fromberg

MISSOURI RIVER COUNTRY

94. Great Plains Dinosaur Museum, Malta

95. Phillips County Museum, Malta
96. Garfield County Museum, Jordan
97. Fort Peck Interpretive Center
98. Valley County Pioneer Museum, Glasgow
99. Daniels County Museum and Pioneer Town, Scobey
100. Montana Cowboy Hall of Fame & Western Heritage Center, Wolf Point
101. Culbertson Museum
102. Fort Union Trading Post National Historic Site, near Sidney
103. MonDak Heritage Center, Sidney
104. McCone County Museum, Circle

SOUTHEAST MONTANA

105. Pictograph Cave State Park, Billings area
106. Western Heritage Center, Billings
107. Moss Mansion Museum, Billings
108. Yellowstone Art Museum, Billings
109. Yellowstone County Museum, Billings
110. Pompeys Pillar National Monument, Billings area
111. Huntley Project Museum
112. Chief Plenty Coups State Park, Pryor
113. Little Bighorn Battlefield National Monument, Crow Agency
114. Custer Battlefield Museum, Garryowen
115. Big Horn County Historical Museum and Visitor Center, Hardin
116. Treasure County 89'ers Museum Complex, Hysham
117. Rosebud County Pioneer Museum, Forsyth
118. Schoolhouse History & Arts Center, Colstrip
119. Jessie Mullin Picture Museum, Lame Deer
120. Cheyenne Indian Museum at Historic St. Labre Indian Mission, Ashland
121. Powder River Historical Museum and Mac's Museum, Broadus
122. WaterWorks Art Museum, Miles City
123. Prairie County Museum and Evelyn Cameron Gallery, Terry
124. Richey Historical Museum
 125. Frontier Gateway Museum, Glendive
126. Makoshika State Park, Glendive
127. Glendive Dinosaur and Fossil Museum
128. O'Fallon Historical Museum, Baker
129. Carter County Museum, Ekalaka

Historical Object:

Notes:

Historical Object:

Notes:

Historical Object:

Notes:

Historical Object:

Notes:

Historical Object:

Notes:

About the Author

Educated as a fine artist, Steph Lehmann has been a professional graphic designer and illustrator for over twenty-eight years. She also has a long history of teaching children fine art and crafts. Steph's the author and illustrator of the award-winning *Who Pooped Field Guide, Journal, and Activity Book* and, more recently, *Who Pooped in the Desert Field Guide, Journal, and Activity Book*. She is also the illustrator of *Jade: Lost in Yellowstone*, all published by Farcountry Press.

AUTHOR'S DEDICATION

To my daughter, Crystal Brust, who spent weekend after weekend working with me on activities for this book. She's always there for me!

And to my mom, Ginny Frankenfield, who nurtured our creativity and was always willing to stay up until the wee hours of the morning making outrageous Halloween costumes, kites that were larger than we were, and any other incredible projects that we dreamed up.

I love you both.

About the Montana Historical Society

The Montana Historical Society was founded in Virginia City in 1865. Since that time, it has served as Montana's memory-keeper. Objects from the Treasure State's past make up its heart and soul. The stories told by these many items intertwine to form a rich tapestry that illustrates our shared past. This children's book is drawn from the Society's publication, *A History of Montana in 101 Objects: Artifacts & Essays from the Montana Historical Society*.

A History of Montana and this companion kids' guide feature only a select few of the "appropriate, curious, and rare" gems from the Society's vast collections. Together, these artifacts help us better understand who we, as Montanans, are today and how we got here. Visit the Montana Historical Society—in person in Helena or online at https://mhs.mt.gov/—to learn even more about Montana's exciting and fascinating past.